CULTURES OF THE WORLD

SOMALIA

Susan M. Hassig

MARSHALL CAVENDISH
New York • London • Sydney

Reference Edition published 1997 by
Marshall Cavendish Corporation
99 White Plains Road
Tarrytown
New York 10591

© Times Editions Pte Ltd 1997

Originated and designed by
Times Books International, an imprint of
Times Editions Pte Ltd

Printed in Singapore

Library of Congress Cataloging-in-Publication Data:
Hassig, Susan M., 1969–
      Somalia / Susan M. Hassig.
          p.   cm. — (Cultures of the world)
      Includes bibliographical references (p.   ) and index.
      Summary: Discusses the geography, history, government,
economy, people, and culture of this peninsular African nation
on the Indian Ocean.
      ISBN 0-7614-0288-8 (lib. bdg.)
      1. Somalia—Juvenile literature. [1. Somalia.]   I. Title.
II. Series.
DT401.5.H37   1997
967.73—dc20   96–20492
                                                        CIP
                                                        AC

INTRODUCTION

ALONG THE EASTERN COAST OF AFRICA lies the peninsula the ancient Egyptians called "God's Land." This is Somalia—a land of deserts, coastal plains, and mountains. Despite years of extreme hardship from drought, famine, and civil war, its people have struggled on, relatively serene. Most Somalis live in close-knit family and clan units. Many of them are nomads with a rich literary tradition, who are well-known for their poetry.

Somalia gained independence from colonial rule in 1960, but for more than 20 years from 1969 to 1991, one man, Mohammed Siad Barre, dominated the country, aligning himself with Soviet powers. Today Somalia is struggling to become a viable nation, free of foreign control for the first time in centuries.

CONTENTS

A girl wearing a typical Somali headscarf.

CONTENTS

A Somali boy selling coconuts.

GEOGRAPHY

SOMALIA'S STRETCH OF COASTLINE is more than 1,860 miles (3,000 km) long. It is washed by the Indian Ocean to the east, with the Gulf of Aden to the north. Over the centuries, millions of settlers and immigrants from the Middle East and elsewhere have come to Somalia through the coastal towns.

The country's total land area is 246,090 square miles (637,370 square km), about the same size as Texas. To Somalia's west and northwest is Ethiopia, to its southwest is Kenya, and in the north is the Republic of Djibouti. The three countries of Somalia, Ethiopia, and Djibouti make up the Horn of Africa.

The terrain of Somalia is mainly one of plains and plateaus, with rugged mountains in the northeast. Coastal plains extend from the lava fields of Djibouti to the southern coastal tip of Somalia. This region, called the Guban, which means "burned from lack of water," lives up to its name. It is a hot and dry area, with very little rainfall or vegetation. Superficial and sand-filled watercourses traverse these coastal plains. During the rainy seasons, the watercourses flow toward the sea, and vegetation begins to sprout. This enables the nomads to bring their herds into the region for grazing. Inland from the coast, the plains are dominated by the steep, northeastern mountains.

The fertile area between the two main rivers, the Jubba and the Shabelle, is another main geographical region.

Opposite: **An area in the Guban, which supports only sparse vegetation.**

Below: **Ocean waves pound the rocks near the capital of Mogadishu.**

7

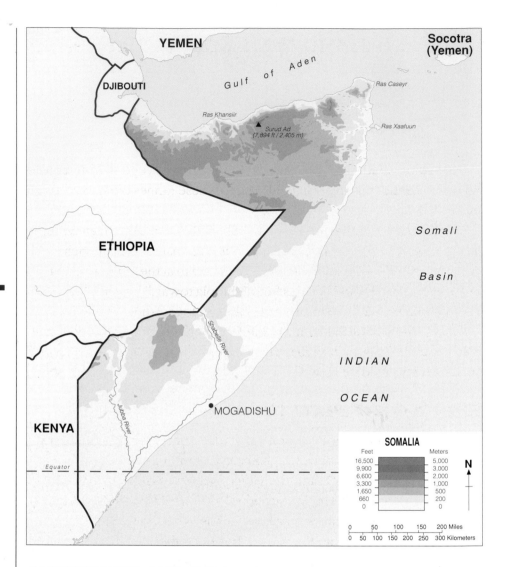

The steep mountains of Somalia rise in the northeast, reaching their highest point of 7,894 feet (2,405 m) at Surud Ad.

MOUNTAINS AND RIVERS

Two mountain ranges—the Oogo and the Golis—rise in the northeast region of Somalia. These rugged ranges extend westward and reach an altitude of 9,000 feet (2,743 m) in the city of Harer in Ethiopia. At Harer, the Oogo and the Golis merge with the Ethiopian highlands.

Somalia's northeast mountains are magnificent, but dangerously precipitous, with an altitude of between 5,900 and 6,890 feet (1,800 and 2,100 m) above sea level.

Extending south from Ethiopia, the mountains level out and become Somalia's central plateau. Annual rainfall in these ranges often exceeds 20 inches (51 cm).

In the southwest, the Jubba and the Shabelle rivers flow from Ethiopia through southern Somalia, carving out expansive valleys rich with vegetation. The Jubba spills into the Indian Ocean at the town of Kismaayo in the south. The Shabelle winds from Ethiopia toward the town of Balcad, about 20 miles (32 km) north of the capital Mogadishu.

Unlike the rest of the country, the fertile area between the two main rivers supports not only verdant grasslands, but forests and abundant wildlife as well.

THE CENTRAL PLATEAU

This major geographical region extends from four corners—Hargeysa (northwest), Gaalkacyo (northeast), the Doollo plains (west), and the Nugaal valley (east). Known as the Haud, this region supports lush vegetation and lakes during the rainy seasons. This is when the Somali nomads move into the region, but since there is no permanent water source, the herdsmen are gone again during the dry season.

Because the Haud extends into Ethiopia, the Somalis and Ethiopians have been in conflict over the rights to pasture in this area since the 1960s. Under an agreement, Ethiopia had been allowing British Somaliland migrants to pasture in its own part of the Haud, but when Somalia gained independence from the British in 1960, Ethiopia no longer wanted to extend this right.

These Somalis are pleased to find a water-hole in the area between the Jubba and Shabelle rivers.

9

The semibarren areas of the north become deserts during the hottest periods of the year.

RAINY AND DRY SEASONS

The climate of Somalia is continuously hot and dry, except at high altitudes and during the main rainy season from April to June when vegetation and grazing pastures flourish. Even the Somali deserts may blossom into colorful displays of flowers at this time of the year.

This three-month season is important to farmers and nomads, but it is also significant for Somalis in general. In addition to providing relief from heat and dryness, or even drought, the rainy season allows people to observe religious ceremonies, get married, or renew contracts or disputes. Many Somalis calculate their age by the number of April-June wet seasons through which they have lived.

The other rainy spell is shorter, lasting only two months from October to November and accounting for about 30% of rainfall.

The first hot season of the year lasts from July to September. Monsoon winds blow parallel to the Somali coast, and very little rain falls. This is the

SELF-DECLARED REPUBLIC OF SOMALILAND

In 1991 the people of the northern region declared themselves independent from Somalia, calling their new state the Republic of Somaliland. This new self-declared nation extends 400 miles (644 km) east of Djibouti, with the Gulf of Aden to the north. In 1992, the Somali national census estimated that 3,875,000 people lived in Somaliland.

This northern region was a British protectorate from 1887. It was captured by the Italians at the start of World War II, but the British reclaimed it toward the end of the war. When Somalia obtained independence from colonial rule in 1960, the former British protectorate joined it to form the United Republic of Somalia.

In the late 1980s rebel groups rose in the north, and launched campaigns to overthrow the national government. After instigating uprisings and civil wars, the northerners declared their independence from Somalia and selected their own head of state.

Somaliland has an interim legislature and a judiciary, and plans are under way for the drafting of a constitution. In 1993 the legislature replaced its first head of state with a new president, Mohammed Ibrahim Egal.

Internationally, Somaliland is not as yet recognized as a sovereign state but still regarded as part of Somalia.

hottest time of the year in the north, but the fresh breezes blowing in from the Indian Ocean provide some cooling relief to the southern coastal regions. The rainy season begins only when the monsoon winds switch directions.

An area of Mogadishu is flooded after heavy rains in April.

The hottest period of the year, especially for the nomads inland, occurs between December and March, when hot dry winds blow throughout the country, often resulting in severe droughts.

Temperatures in Somalia range from highs of 86–104° F (30–40° C) to lows of 32° F (0° C). In the north, the climate varies from freezing cold in December to scorching heat in July. Humidity fluctuates from 40% during the afternoon to almost 85% at night. Along the coast, the humidity level stays at about 70% throughout the year.

SPARSE VEGETATION

Due to the scarcity of rainfall, vegetation is rather sparse in Somalia, except for the areas along the Jubba and Shabelle rivers. Trees native to the dry highlands are the boswellia and commiphora. Frankincense and myrrh, renowned since Biblical times, are the aromatic products of these trees.

In most of the country, low trees such as acacia cover patches of short grass, desert, and sand dunes. The mountainous region supports a wider variety of vegetation, including aloe plants and remnants of juniper forests at altitudes exceeding 4,920 feet (1,500 m).

The strange sight of a towering termites' nest, reaching nearly as high as a tree.

PLENTIFUL WILDLIFE

In contrast to this largely desert landscape, wildlife is plentiful. The largest animals are the lion, cheetah, leopard, elephant, buffalo, zebra, giraffe, and hippopotamus. The male lions that roam the central region can exceed nine feet (2.7 m) in length, and have either black or tawny manes. The cheetah, the fastest mammal on earth, has a golden or gray coat with black spots, and a white belly. Unfortunately, hunters have killed off all the rhinoceros in Somalia and most of east Africa, and even the elephant is in danger of being wiped out.

Also inhabiting Somalia's semiarid regions are donkey, sheep, gazelle, giraffe, and antelope. The species of giraffe native to Somalia is the

reticulated giraffe, which has a reddish-brown coat and either two or three horns. Small antelopes, known as dik-diks, live in the north and along the Jubba and Shabelle rivers. The name dik-dik comes from the sound made by the animal. A dik-dik is only 12 inches (30 cm) high at the shoulders, with a soft, gray coat. The male dik-dik has small horns often covered by a patch of hair. The dik-dik is the emblem of the Somali police.

Quite a sight on the Somali plains are the great big nests of termites that look like small hills. These towering nests are solid structures of hard-baked earth, formed by the insects' saliva and droppings.

The pink flamingo and the hoopoe are among Somalia's most colorful birds. The hoopoe has pinkish-brown feathers, with black-and-white stripes. Its crested head has been featured in many ancient Egyptian drawings. According to Somali storytellers, the hoopoe used to have a golden crest, but these bright African birds begged King Solomon to change their crests to a chestnut shade—because too many people were killing them for their gold.

Colorful birds like the pink flamingo are found in the riverine areas of the south.

POETRY OF THE CAMEL

The most important animal to the Somalis is the camel—so important that many poems and songs have been written about it. Traditionally, the most noble calling in Somalia is camel herding. The richer a family becomes, the more camels it will buy. Indeed, a family's standing in the community is often measured by the number of camels it owns.

Somalis not only use camels to transport themselves and their possessions, but they also slaughter the animals for religious festivities. They also exchange camels as a symbol for mending a broken relationship or for cultivating a friendship.

HOW THE LEOPARD GOT ITS SPOTS

The leopard is the symbol of Somalia and appears on government stamps and parade flags. These lithe and beautiful animals live in the north, along the northeast coast, and near the Jubba River, sharing their habitat with the lion and the cheetah. Leopards have long been coveted for their hides, but leopard hunting is now prohibited.

Somalis like to tell the story of the leopard and the man from Ethiopia, the neighboring country in the west. This tale has also been told by the English writer Rudyard Kipling.

It seems that the Ethiopian was out hunting one day with a leopard by his side. "You are an incredible hunter," said the man to the leopard. "The only thing is, all the animals can spot you from miles away. That's because your coat is as bright as a sunflower!"

"Well, do something about it then," said the leopard. "How about putting some spots on my body? That will help me blend in with the foliage. But just make sure you don't make the spots too vulgar-big, as I have no wish to look like the giraffe."

The Ethiopian smiled and obliged by pressing his fingers to his own dark skin, and then putting his fingertips on the leopard's skin. Wherever he touched the leopard, there appeared five little marks, close together.

Several times the man's fingers slipped, and the marks came out somewhat blurred, sort of all blending into each other.

That is why to this day, say the Somalis, there are always five small black spots close together on the leopard's coat, and why some black spots look much bigger.

The hippo, which looks harmless enough, may sometimes attack a person venturing into the water. But Somalis run a greater risk from the wild buffalo, which may charge at the slightest disturbance.

NOMADIC AND TOWN LIFE

Somalia is known to many as a nation of nomads. More than 65% of the population of over eight million live in the rural areas and most of them follow a way of life that has remained unchanged for centuries. Because water sources are so scarce, Somali nomads are constantly on the move, roaming the country with their flocks of sheep, goats, and camels in search of water and new pastures.

A Somali nomad and his herd of goats.

Once they find a suitable place to stay for some time, they rebuild their makeshift homes from sticks and animal skins that are carried on the backs of camels or donkeys.

The nomads themselves often travel with nothing more than the clothes on their backs, a bowl for food or water, a staff for herding, and a headrest for their sleep at night.

Most Somali nomads live in the highlands and plateaus during the dry months, moving up to the Haud during the rainy periods. They set up small temporary settlements in the Haud near dependable sources of water. When the water runs out, they return to the highlands until the next rainy season.

Some nomads have taken to growing crops in the areas by the Jubba and Shabelle rivers. When the rains come, these seminomadic groups move inland to raise their herds; when the rains cease, they move back to their farms beside the rivers.

The rest of the population live in small towns and cities, many of them along the eastern coast facing the Indian Ocean.

MOGADISHU This is the national capital and the largest city in Somalia. In the ninth century Arab and Persian traders founded a colony here, establishing it as a trading port for gold from southcentral Africa. Its name means "the seat of the Shah," a reflection of Persian influence. It continues to serve as a central port.

HARGEYSA Located on a broad plateau in the north, Hargeysa is an important center for livestock trading. It was the capital of the British protectorate of Somaliland.

KISMAAYO Lying southwest of Mogadishu on the eastern coast, Kismaayo is the third largest city. It first arose as a religious community in the 19th century. Many of its inhabitants have jobs in industry or fishing.

BERBERA Arab geographers first mentioned this city in the 13th century. It is situated on the northern coast and is still an important port, with strong links with Aden and Saudi Arabian posts.

HISTORY

DURING EARLY EGYPTIAN TIMES, Persian, Greek, Roman, and Egyptian seafarers called at Somali coastal ports and loaded their ships with frankincense, myrrh, rhinoceros horn, and ivory. Some of the merchants eventually came to live in this land.

Centuries before, the Somali people themselves were already established inland. Many believe they are descendants of Noah's son Ham, who crossed the Red Sea and married an original inhabitant of the Horn of Africa. Other scholars believe that Somalis were actually descendants of the nomads of Ethiopia.

After the sixth century, foreign traders settled along the Gulf of Aden. The present town of Zeila was once a walled enclave called Seylac, known for its coffee and slave trading. Muslim merchants began to set up home in Seylac, bringing their religion to the area. By the ninth century, Arab and Persian traders had founded a colony for handling and shipping gold at the modern-day city of Mogadishu.

Above: **Persian traders of the 14th century. Many of these Muslim merchants had settled in Somalia by then.**

Opposite: **The minaret of the Ali Hussein mosque in Mogadishu.**

EARLY SOMALI TRIBES

Two distinct tribes were living in Somalia by the 12th century. These were the Samaale and the Sab tribes, each with its own language and culture. The Samaales had no chief or court, but were ruled by an assembly of men who met occasionally. The Sabs had a central leader who had control over large areas. This tribe lived in the southern regions and was mostly engaged in herding, trading, or growing crops.

19

SPREAD OF THE MUSLIM FAITH

The Muslim faith and its cultural beliefs were spreading from the coastal towns to the interior by the 11th century, following the arrival of an important Muslim chief from Arabia. Sheikh Jabarti was head of the Darod Somali, a tribal people that were already settled in the northeast corner of the Somali peninsula. In the 13th century, the Muslim faith expanded further inland. Another Muslim leader had arrived, and was to prove just as influential as Sheikh Jabarti before him. This was Sheikh Isaq , who soon founded the Isaq Somali clan.

Just as the Darod Somali had done, the Isaq Somali clan grew in numbers. Both clans integrated with the local Samaale and Sab tribes by marriage, and made further inroads from the coastal towns.

In the 15th century, the Muslim population became involved in a long struggle with Christians from the kingdom of Abyssinia, or present-day Ethiopia. Battles were fought, with Somali tribesmen often forming part of the Muslim armies. Relations between the two lands had until then been one of tolerance, because Abyssinian Christians had protected Muslim refugees from Mecca during the seventh century.

An ambitious Abyssinian leader, Yeshaq, successfully invaded a Somali town in 1415. He then directed his courtiers to compose a victory hymn, and the song that resulted is the first written record of Somalia.

Nearly 100 years went by before the Muslims were able to recover from their defeat. But eventually they gathered their forces and invaded the towns of Abyssinia.

A Persian hunter of the late 14th century. By the 15th century, Muslims settled in Somalia were engaged in a fierce struggle with the Abyssinian Christians from Ethiopia.

WEALTH OF THE COASTAL TOWNS

Mogadishu first became an urban center in the ninth century. By the 14th century it had become a major town with a congregational Muslim mosque, a theological school, and a palace. The Muslim traveler Ibn Battuta visited the city in 1331 and recorded that a Somali sultan ruled the city with the aid of ministers, legal experts, and commanders. He also portrayed Mogadishu citizens as rich and fat.

During the next two centuries, Mogadishu and other coastal trading cities prospered. But centers of power shifted as the population migrated toward the interior. The inland kingdom of Ujuuraan that arose is a notable example. This powerful kingdom came to an end in the 17th century, unable to withstand internal strife, nomadic invasions, and Portuguese interference with commerce. The Portuguese were eventually ousted from the country, but other European powers invaded in the 1800s and changed the course of the country forever.

The sultan of Ujuuraan was one of the first in the land to use slave labor. It appears that he ordered Bantu-speaking farmers to be captured as slaves—because he could not get native Somalis to do the farming. Slaves were bartered and exchanged for ivory, rhinoceros horn, and delicate woods and later became an important part of the economy.

Mogadishu flourished in the 14th century, and continued to prosper over the next two centuries.

21

FOREIGN INTEREST IN SOMALIA

The battle for control over Somalia in the 19th century involved Great Britain, Italy, and France, with Egypt and Ethiopia also wanting a stake. In 1840, Britain annexed Aden, a land across the Red Sea in Arabia, and entered into two treaties with Somali sultanates to supply cattle to Somalia.

By 1869 the Egyptians were occupying towns along the north coast. In 1874 the British stopped Egypt from controlling towns on the northeastern coast, and vice-consuls were assigned to several of these towns, but the Egyptians managed to establish a powerful cultural influence in Berbera and Seylac that lasted for many years.

In 1884 the British drove the Egyptians from Somalia, signed treaties with the Somali clans, and set up a protectorate along the coast. Meanwhile, Italy was concentrating on Somalia's neighbor, Ethiopia, which later became an Italian protectorate. Eventually the Italians reached the British coastal protectorate.

A British explorer presents his kills to a tribal chief in Somalia in the 19th century.

In 1891 and 1894, two treaties were signed by Britain and Italy, specifying the boundaries of their influence. Ethiopia was excluded from the negotiations, even though the two colonial powers were dividing up Ethiopian territories. Ethiopia objected to the treaties and forced Italy to redefine its boundaries in 1897. Several of the ports on the Somalia coast that the British controlled were leased to the Italians in the early 1800s. This led to Italian dominance in southern Somalia, subsequently known as Italian Somaliland. The third European presence, the French, had established a colony in the north of Somalia by the middle of the 19th century.

This European control was a source of great dissatisfaction and resentment among the local Somalis. A Muslim leader, Mohammed bin Abdullah, appealed to the people to join him in a *jihad*, or holy war, against the European Christians. He began his campaign by forming an army in the northern coastal town of Berbera.

This Muslim leader was highly respected, even venerated, by his disciples, but the European Christians dismissed him as a fanatic. The European settlers later discovered, to their high cost, that they had greatly underestimated him. The "Mad Mullah," as he came to be known, fought and massacred thousands of them. In 1910 the British withdrew from the Somali interior after losing about a third of their men in battles.

During World War I the Germans and Turks supported Mohammed in his fight against the British. But in 1920 the British bombed Mohammed's camp, forcing him to surrender or to flee. Mohammed fled and died a natural death later that year.

The picture below was headlined "The Mad Mullah's soldiers: some of the dervishes who have been terrorizing Somaliland" by a British newspaper on August 16, 1913. It subsequently turned out that the report was falsified, as the men in the picture, reported as Somalis attacking the town of Burao, were not Somalis at all but Zulus, who would not have been anywhere near Burao.

Two British officers of the early 19th century purchasing sheep and goats from the Somalis.

COLONIAL POWERS AT WAR

When World War II broke out in 1939, the two colonial powers in Somalia, Britain and Italy, were on opposite sides. The two countries concentrated their efforts on the war in Europe, but they also fought each other in Somalia.

The British formed battalion units in their colonized settlements, and the Italians organized themselves in the south. In August 1940, the Italians invaded and captured British Somaliland. But the British, swift to retaliate, reclaimed their protectorate and occupied the Italian territories.

The British then sent military administrators to govern their extensive colonies in the Somali peninsula. They moved their capital from Berbera to Hargeysa and brought about political and cultural changes. They opened nonreligious or secular schools, reorganized the court system, improved the working conditions of agricultural workers, and created district and provincial councils.

AIMS OF THE EARLY POLITICAL GROUPS

The first political organization in Somalia was started in 1943 as a reaction against European colonization. It was called the Somali Youth Club (SYC), and its first members were 13 Somalis from five of the six clan families.

A large group of Somali police officers, whom the British had trained, also joined the SYC. This was encouraged by the British, who believed it would help combat the growing Italian influence. By 1946 over 25,000 Somalis belonged to the SYC, and the organization spread from Mogadishu to British Somaliland, Ethiopia, and Kenya.

A year later the group changed its name to the Somali Youth League (SYL) and focused on unifying local territories and protecting Somali interests. It also aimed at developing a modern educational system and a written Somali language. Although the founding members were from the main Somali clans, the SYL worked toward the growth of a strong national identity and the elimination of clan divisions.

The SYL acted as a spur to others to form political groups. The Patriotic Benefit Union, later called the Hizbia Digil-Mirifle Somali (HDMS), emerged during the late 1940s.

The HDMS included agricultural clans from the fertile region between the rivers Jubba and Shabelle. It regarded the British-influenced SYL as a rival group and consequently accepted help from the Italians, including cash donations.

The ruin of an Italian building of the early 19th century.

The British retained control but allowed the Italians to form political groups, which led to a resurgence of Italian strength in the region.

By the end of World War II, the Allied powers decreed that Britain need not return any Italian colony that it had captured. Eventually in 1949 the Council of Foreign Ministers in Europe allowed Italy to govern its Somali colony, but only under United Nations supervision.

The Roman arch of the Catholic cathedral in Mogadishu is one of the city's more imposing structures, attesting to the strength of the Italian presence before World War II.

ROAD TO INDEPENDENCE

The Allied powers had allowed Italy to regain its sphere of control in Somalia. But there was a major condition attached—Italy had to help Somalia become independent by 1960. In this process of preparing for independence, the youth groups were to play an important part.

ITALIAN SOMALILAND Of all the young political groups that contested the 1954 municipal elections in Italian Somaliland, the Somali Youth League was the most successful, obtaining 48% of the vote. The HDMS received 22%, and the other 20 parties shared 30%.

In the general election of 1956, the SYL once again received the most votes, enabling it to put 43 of its members in the 60-seat legislature.

The HDMS won 13 seats, and the Somali Democratic Party obtained three seats. This staggering victory of the SYL discouraged other smaller groups from forming, and many existing parties ended up joining the SYL instead.

In 1959 the SYL resorted to drastic measures in order to gain full control before independence in 1960. It arrested hundreds of members from rival groups and closed down many of their headquarters. Consequently the party won 83 out of 90 seats in the 1959 elections.

The SYL then attempted to balance the conflicting interests of its clan members, which was a problem area both within and outside the party.

BRITISH SOMALILAND   Unlike the Italians, the British prohibited Somalis from forming political parties until they had obtained independence. The first British Somaliland election was held in 1959. But the Somaliland National League (SNL) refused to take part, as its leaders were convinced that the British would rig the election.

The second election occurred in February 1960. The SNL not only participated, but won 20 out of 33 legislative seats. The Somali Youth League did not win a single seat in this election.

Britain decided, in a surprise move in April 1960, that it would grant independence to its British colony a few days after Italian Somaliland had become independent. This led Somali leaders in the north and south to meet, in an attempt to unify the two territories as one nation before the momentous occasion in July 1960.

The museum in Mogadishu, once the palace of the Sultan of Zanzibar, used to be beautifully maintained, but now looks rather rundown.

27

GREAT SOMALI FAMINE THAT TOUCHED THE WORLD

A delicate balance of life and death hangs over a desert country such as Somalia. Every living thing depends on the rains for its existence. When the rains ceased between the years of 1978 and 1981, Somalia suffered a devastating drought. The world saw pictures of animal carcasses strewn over the desert sands, and worse still, the unforgettable images of people starving to death.

In answer to the country's desperate call for help, 17 international relief organizations went into action. Save the Children Fund, International Christian Relief, and Action Aid among others flew their relief workers to the worst drought-stricken areas to set up refugee camps.

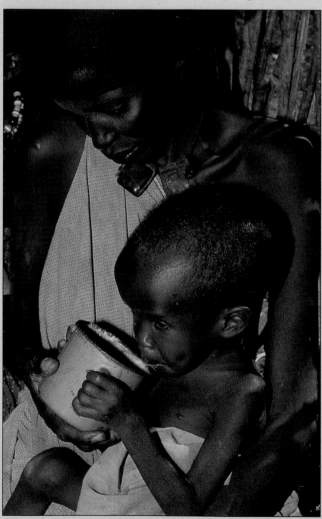

The scenes that greeted the relief groups went beyond their worst expectations. They found the Somalis, many of them children, in advanced states of starvation or malnourishment and suffering from malaria, tuberculosis, and other lung infections. There was a dire lack of sanitation, medicine, food, water, and other necessities.

Somalis from all over the country walked for miles to arrive at the refugee camps. Extra food was given to emaciated children, pregnant women, nursing mothers, the elderly, and the sick. Everyone else received small rations of food twice a day. Volunteers also supplied medication, tents, and toilets, as well as vehicles and educational materials where appropriate.

The devastating drought finally ended in 1981 when the rains came. But this brought a new crisis in the form of floods. The parched ground could not absorb the rainfall, and there was no vegetation left from the drought to stop the rush of water over the land.

So, despite the rains, Somalis continued to die of malnutrition.

FREE BUT RIPE FOR REVOLUTION

As planned, the British and Italians freed their hold on Somalia in July 1960. The northern and southern regions finally became the independent nation of Somalia. Although it was a joy to the Somali people to have the colonial yoke finally thrown off, ahead of them lay other obstacles to true independence. The new leaders were faced with the formidable task of unifying two territories of people who spoke two distinct languages, held different political views, operated different educational systems, and had separate currencies.

To assist in the task of unification, the United Nations appointed a Commission for Integration to merge the laws and cultures of the two regions. But tension between the clans of the north and south continued, leading to warfare and political revolutions. Within a few years of independence, Somalia was to come under Communist rule.

Mercenaries guard a building during the warfare that exploded between north and south in Somalia.

29

GOVERNMENT

THE NEW GOVERNMENT OF 1960 drafted and adopted a constitution that was meant to unify the two regions formerly controlled by Italy and Britain. Mogadishu was chosen as the new capital—a move that angered the northern Somalis, who did not want a southern town to be the capital.

The first president of Somalia was Aden Abdullah Osman and the first prime minister was Abdi Rashid Al Shermarke. In 1963, the two leaders formed the Democratic Republic of Somalia. Despite this attempt at unification, the tension between north and south continued.

The country held national elections in 1964 and reelected Osman as president, but Osman did not keep Shermarke as his prime minister. Instead he appointed Abdirazak Haji Hussein, who appealed to the younger Somalis. Osman then picked an entirely new group of individuals for his cabinet, in the hope of solving deep-seated national problems.

Shermarke remained bitter toward Osman and ran against him for president in 1967. Shermarke won and appointed a northerner, Mohammed Ibrahim Egal, as prime minister.

Egal tried hard to improve relations with other African countries and with the United States. He did succeed in strengthening Somalia's relationship with Kenya and Ethiopia, which led to commercial and telecommunication links between the countries. Somali nomads were also allowed to bring their flocks once more into Ethiopia for grazing.

Opposite: **The monument to independence in Mogadishu.**

Below: **A painting featuring most of the African heads of state in 1974. The occasion, a summit conference in Mogadishu that year, was a high point in the political life of the nation.**

Mohammed Siad Barre, who took control of the country and proceeded to rule it with an iron hand.

COUP OF OCTOBER 1969

The man who regained power in 1967, President Shermarke, was shot and killed by one of his bodyguards—apparently for political and tribal reasons. Prime Minister Egal immediately appointed a northerner and a Darod clan member as president. This political move infuriated the southerners and spurred them on to revolt.

On October 21, 1969, southern armies captured Mogadishu and abducted government leaders. The commander of the army, Major General Mohammed Siad Barre, the leader of this combined army and police coup, placed a tank outside Egal's house and assumed control of the country, declaring himself head of state. Western powers suspected the Soviet Union to be behind the coup, because Siad Barre and his fellow revolutionaries immediately adopted Communism as the form of government.

Siad Barre was tough and ruthless. He threw out the Somali Constitution, banned all political parties, and abolished the National Assembly. His government openly toed the Soviet line and began to broadcast Communist messages on street corners. Every home was required to display a portrait or photograph of President Siad Barre. Even artists and poets were forced to incorporate Communist propaganda into their work.

SEVERING OF SOVIET LINKS

With Communism as the central form of government, Somalia was seen as a "Soviet satellite" by the West. Siad Barre remained firmly in power, surviving all attempts to remove him. In 1971, one of his vice-presidents and a senior member of parliament planned to have him assassinated, but the plot was foiled.

Siad Barre's friendship with the Soviets was severely strained during the 1970s. As part of his attempt to win disputed territory within Ethiopia, he encouraged a military group called the Western Somali Liberation Front (WSLF) to attack Ethiopian troops along the border. This became known as the Ogaden War, and for two years WSLF troops continued to invade Ethiopia and cut off its contact with the outside world. Somewhat surprisingly, the Soviet Union supported Ethiopia in this war, rather than its "satellite." This so enraged Siad Barre that he ordered Soviet advisors in his country to leave within one day. The Ogaden War continued until 1978. Civilian suffering was widespread and the economy was left in a bad state.

Siad Barre was finally forced to seek help from other countries. Eventually the United States, Britain, Egypt, Italy, and Saudi Arabia came to his aid, but stipulated that he was not to turn to the Soviets again.

Propaganda posters of the 1970s outside a government office serve to remind the nation of who was still firmly in power.

A U.S. soldier eats his rations during guard duty, watched by a Somali boy.

When Siad Barre fled in early 1991, he left the country in a state of anarchy. Civil war was raging, the economy was crippled, and all foreign aid had been cut off because of Somalia's poor human rights record.

DOWNFALL OF SIAD BARRE

In 1979, on the tenth anniversary of his military coup, Siad Barre announced that Somalia was to be a Socialist state. His brand of Socialism was a loose combination of Muslim principles and influences from Marx, Lenin, Mao, and Mussolini.

Yet the country fared no better over the next decade. Droughts and civil wars took their toll, despite the foreign aid that came in. The northern Somali clans, bitterly opposed to southern leadership, were waiting for an opportunity to revolt.

Northerners, led by the Somali National Movement, instigated uprisings in Mogadishu and other southern cities in May and June of 1988. Siad Barre, unable to prevent these attacks, resorted to bombing the rebels by air. This effectively stopped the uprisings, but it also destroyed much of the southern cities. Cities in the north were also bombed, with Hargeysa suffering the worst casualties.

By 1990, U.S. troops entered Somalia, to try and control the fighting between north and south and to relieve the suffering of the civilian population. The presence of U.S. forces led to several events that made international headlines. News pictures, for instance, showed Somali troops driving through the streets of Mogadishu, dragging the body of a U.S. soldier behind their vehicle.

The United States was quick to dispatch helicopters to Somalia on January 5, 1991, to rescue Americans and other foreigners. Weeks later, on January 27, Siad Barre and his supporters fled Mogadishu. Most Somalis were relieved at this outcome, but because Siad Barre had been such a dominating presence in the 21 years or so of his rule, the civilian population felt lost without a leader.

This group belongs to a force loyal to General Aidid.

UNITED NATIONS FORCES

A year after the collapse of Siad Barre's government, the United Nations sent troops to Somalia. The man with power in the south was General Mohammed Aidid, leader of the United Somali Congress, a force formerly loyal to Siad Barre.

Aidid, opposed to Western military intervention, accused the United Nations of aiding Somali guerrillas. In order to prevent another international incident that might endanger U.N. forces in Somalia, the U.N. representative in Mogadishu resigned.

In 1994 the United States deployed fresh troops to Somalia, persuading Aidid to sign a peace treaty with his rivals from the north. This peace was short-lived. The United States' subsequent attempt to have Aidid removed from power and tried for various war crimes was unsuccessful.

Forced to flee from their home in 1993, this family of four still retains a certain dignity.

APPALLING HUMAN RIGHTS

The main clans in power by 1992 were the Somali National Alliance and the Somali Salvation Alliance. The other clans with some control were the Hawiye and Darod clans and the Habre Gedir and Abgal sub-clans. There was a further deterioration in human rights for the civilian population. Killings, kidnap, rape, and other atrocities were inflicted daily on ordinary Somalis in the warfare between north and south.

Foreign peacekeeping troops continued to sustain casualties. In 1993 for instance, Somali soldiers attacked a group of Pakistani soldiers in the U.N. peacekeeping force, leaving 18 dead. By the middle of 1994, only 50 U.S. soldiers still remained in Somalia. All other Western troops had been recalled by their countries by then.

In 1994, the economy took a turn for the better, the result of good rainfall and bountiful harvests. Many displaced Somalis were able to return to their homes. Despite this improved outlook, the civil wars continued.

Peacekeeping forces of the United Nations continued to remain in Somalia until March 1995. By then Aidid and some of his opponents were trying to reach some sort of agreement, but the self-proclaimed Republic of Somaliland remained recalcitrant.

VICTIMS OF CLAN RIVALRY AND CIVIL WARS

Because Somalis have always shown ultimate loyalty to their clans and sub-clans, they complied when clan leaders issued them guns and other weapons and sent them to war. Even young children were carrying weapons by the early 1990s. The United Nations estimated that 1.5 million Somali civilians were armed in 1993.

United Nations figures also showed that tens of thousands of Somalis have died as a result of clan warfare in the years following Siad Barre's departure in 1991. Many of these deaths, up to 3,000 daily in the year 1992, were from starvation and malnutrition. The chief victims in the clan warfare were women and children, some of whom were involved in actual combat. Boys as young as 14 were made to take part in major clan warfare.

Rival clans have met several times and signed peace treaties but with no positive result. The United Nations has also intervened and passed several resolutions to try and end the fighting and to improve human rights for civilians.

In addition, the United Nations tried to build up a national police force but the clans continue to control local laws. Some of the clans have established Islamic courts, which apply strict Islamic law for the general population. These courts impose severe punishments for offenders, such as cutting off a hand for theft.

ECONOMY

SOMALIA'S STATUS REMAINS that of a Third World country. In the years since independence from colonial rule in 1960, the economy has picked up only slightly. The basis of the economy continues to be agriculture and animal herding.

The public sector played a dominant role when Siad Barre implemented his Socialist concepts and abolished private ownership of banks, insurance companies, and wholesale trade. By 1989 there was rampant inflation and soaring food prices. Wages in the towns and cities stagnated.

By 1992, after the collapse of the Socialist government, Western powers were once again supplying aid to the country, and the economy of several cities improved. A notable example is the town of Baydhabo, northwest of Mogadishu. Before 1992 Somalis called Baydhabo the "City of Death" because over 300 people died every day from malnutrition and starvation. With the help of the United Nations, Baydhabo's citizens have replanted their farms and raised enough crops to feed themselves. Unfortunately, the rest of the country has not done as well.

Left: **A bustling scene, as these settled nomads collect the corn harvest in sacks for the wholesale traders.**

Opposite: **Two women pick a crop of grapefruit in an orchard in the town of Marka.**

Sacks of grain have just been unloaded at the quayside in Mogadishu harbor.

SELF-HELP PROGRAMS

During the years of colonial rule, exporting bananas was Somalia's main source of foreign income. In addition, the Italians had helped to set up alcohol distilleries and a sugarcane plantation. In British Somaliland, the economy revolved around the breeding and raising of livestock.

On independence, the government came up with the First Five-Year Plan, which counted heavily on foreign aid. But economic aid was not as forthcoming as expected, and the Short-Term Development Program was drafted.

Within three years, this plan did succeed in several ways. It improved administration, mobilized domestic resources, and created more favorable economic conditions. Enterprises and projects created included a cotton textile plant, fisheries, meat canneries, a milk plant, deepwater ports, and paved roads to transport bananas.

After October 1969, Siad Barre's government emphasized self-help and self-reliance in its economic strategy. Land was requisitioned for agricultural purposes, but Siad Barre kept his promise to the nomads that he would not take their camels.

The economy improved during the Socialist programs of the early 1970s. Milk factories were restructured to raise production, and plants were built to manufacture cigarettes, matches, cardboard boxes, wheat flour, pasta, and polythene bags.

Sugar factories were expanded and a fishery operation in Kismaayo was opened. But none of this was sufficient, and the government had to resort to borrowing money from other countries—first from the Soviet Union and then from the United States and other Western nations.

Fish are plentiful along the Somali coast, but it was only in the 1970s that commercial fishing began to be taken seriously.

FISHERIES DOING WELL

Many types of fish live on the rocky sea bottom along the seemingly endless stretch of Somali coast. The most common fish are anchovy, sardine, tuna, herring, and mackerel. Other plentiful varieties are flounder, snapper, shark, sea ray, spiny lobster, oyster, octopus, and clam.

Despite this easy availability, Somalis on the whole are not great fish eaters. Because of this, the country did not seriously engage in commercial fishing until the 1970s. Fishing became a profitable concern under the Socialist government and is continuing to do well.

Fishing cooperatives were created in 1974 to purchase boats and fishing gear and to look after the handling and marketing aspects. Cooperatives in the big coastal cities were encouraged to sell most of their fresh fish directly. Any fish left unsold were salted and purchased by the government agency Somalfish, set up to promote the fishing industry.

RURAL AND CITY WORK

Over 82% of the population is employed in agriculture, forestry, and fishing. The farmers in the south grow crops such as corn, bananas, and other fruits. Those in the north cultivate wheat, barley, tomatoes, potatoes, onions, cabbage, fruit, and coffee. Bananas are the main export crop and the country's major money-earner, after livestock.

Many Somalis also work in forestry, cutting down trees or working in factories that process the trees into wood for furniture or boats.

SOMALIA'S CROPS, NATIVE AND FOREIGN

Coffee and cotton are native to Somalia, but many other crops are grown. Corn and peanuts were introduced into the country in the 19th century by Americans, and banana plants were brought in by Asian settlers. Today the chief crop is bananas, a large green variety that grows on trees with dark, shiny leaves.

Coffee is grown on plantations. The plants give out a fragrance when they blossom in January and February. The coffee beans, first green and then turning to red, are called cherries because they resemble berries on the coffee plant.

Cotton thrives in the drier regions of the country. The plant is a knee-high bush that produces white, fluffy bolls at harvest time. After they are picked, Somali farmers send the cotton bolls to a factory called a ginnery for processing.

Peanuts grow below ground on the roots of the plants, which is why they are also called groundnuts. Somalis harvest them by pulling the entire plant out of the earth.

With the growth of the cities over the last few decades, many Somalis left the traditional fields of farming and herding animals for business and professional careers. But not many Somali women are involved in this process of urbanization.

Economic life in the cities tends to be relaxed and casual. Businessmen spend almost as much time at the coffee house as in the office, regarding the coffee shop as a place to meet, discuss politics, exchange money, and keep up contacts.

Three Somali children prepare the ground for planting corn in the next season.

AGRICULTURE AND LIVESTOCK

In years of good harvests, cotton, sesame, groundnuts, and sorghum are exported. In the 1970s and 1980s, agricultural cooperatives were set up in the country. The government acquired the land of several farmers to combine it all into one big farm, but each farmer shared in the work of the cooperative.

Such cooperatives worked well for a while, but the Somalis soon became tired of working so hard for something they did not own and could not pass on to their children. A special government group is trying to raise money for heavy farm equipment to replace outdated manual tools in order to promote agricultural growth.

Much of the country's livestock is exported to Egypt and Saudi Arabia. Tens of thousands of animals died in the severe droughts of the 1980s, but the numbers of cattle, sheep, and goats have risen again, due to the diligent efforts of the Somalis in caring for their livestock.

Food aid arriving at Mogadishu airport in 1992.

INDUSTRIAL GROWTH

There has been some industrial growth in Somalia over the past few decades. Foreign nations have set up fisheries, tanneries, pharmaceutical plants, sugar refineries, and petroleum and uranium mining facilities. With the help of the Soviets in the 1970s, the government built five large plants for meat, dairy, and fish processing. By the late 1970s, the state owned 53 large and modern manufacturing industries.

After World War II, deposits of petroleum and natural gas were discovered in Somalia. But the commercial extraction of these natural resources was restricted until 1981.

Somalia has since joined efforts with Jordan to explore 22,000 square miles (57,000 square km) for uranium and iron ore. In the 1980s, geologists working near Berbera found what they believe to be one of the world's largest gypsum-anhydrite deposits.

DONKEY CARTS TO AIRPLANES

Somalia's status as a Third World country is evident in its poorly developed road and rail system. There are not enough railways to connect the major cities and towns. From the early 1970s onward, Somalia has built hundreds of roads to try and improve the transportation system.

Somalis favor four-wheel drive vehicles and motorcycles for road transport. In the cities they also travel by bus, taxi, and private car. But many town and city dwellers travel by foot or in a donkey cart. Even in the largest cities people walk down the streets with their goats, camels, and cattle.

The capital Mogadishu has an international airport, and other cities such as Hargeysa have small domestic airports.

THE MEDIA

Although Somalia is the size of Texas, it has only three radio stations and one television station. Until the overthrow of Siad Barre, the government controlled radio and television programming and broadcast political messages around the country. Being a relatively young nation that lacked its own language until independence, radio and television were the means to a universal language. Today, television broadcasts are transmitted in Somali and Arabic for two hours each day, with an additional hour on Friday.

Somalia has several newspapers printed in Somali, Arabic, Italian, and English. The Socialist government used to control the newspapers and censored their contents. Today, most newspapers are small pamphlets promoting membership in a clan or political group. The Somalis obtain international news largely through the British Broadcasting Corporation's daily radio program.

The driver of this old truck stuck on a beach is fortunate to have willing helpers. The lack of a proper road system in many parts of Somali means drivers must use what access they can in getting from one spot to another.

SOMALIS

SOMALIS ARE PEOPLE from a similar genealogical line. Most of them are tall and slim and have beautiful features. Nomadic Somalis believe that they originate from a common father named Samalle (or Ham), who was the son of the Biblical Noah. All Somalis belong to one or another of the six clans or tribes in the country.

Over 85% of the population is Somali, while the remaining 15% is Bantu, Arab, European, or Asian. There are about eight million people living in Somalia, with 33 inhabitants per square mile (13 per square km). Due to the poverty and civil strife, average life expectancy is only 47.1 years. Women on average live to 48.6 years, men to only 45.4 years. Nearly half the population are under the age of 14, while slightly over half are between 15 and 64 years of age. The rest, about 2%, are over the age of 65.

Opposite: **Somali woman and her child.**

Below: **Nomadic women putting up an** *akal,* **a traditional home made of sticks and animal skins.**

Somalis are a family-oriented people; they place great importance on their relatives, line of descent, and clan membership. Children learn early about their lineage and clan associations.

Somalia has been called a "nation of poets," as most Somalis share a great love of poetry. They also believe strongly in their traditional way of life. This, more than anything else, has enabled them to endure the difficult years of colonialism, tyranny, civil war, and famine.

CLAN SOCIAL SYSTEM

Somalia's social system centers around their clans. There are six primary clans or tribes—the Dir, Darod, Isaq, and Hawiye of the north; the Digil and Rahanwayn of the south. These clans are constantly at war with each other, over north-south rivalry. A Somali's allegiance is always first to his or her immediate family, followed by the immediate lineage, then the clan of lineage, and finally the clan family.

To function as a member of the Somali social system, a person must belong to a clan. Arabs and Persians who have migrated to Somalia often invent a fictitious clan background to try and fit in, and foreign visitors often feel left out in this tight-knit society.

The clan system is deep-rooted and exercises an inescapable and powerful influence on the political and social life of the nation.

Two men from the same clan. Men with clan ties are obliged to respect these bonds.

CLAN ALLIANCE

When the clan families became too large for their leaders to manage, sub-clans developed. Eventually the clans and sub-clans devised contracts to determine the rights and obligations of their members. For instance, one clan would sign a contract with another clan to join forces for political or military purposes.

The clans also unite to seek revenge on someone who has injured or murdered one of their members. As in the nature of contracts, these agreements are only for a certain period, after which each clan is free to form alliances with other tribes.

These nomads belong to a pastoral clan. They move widely in the northern regions and in the south between the Jubba and the Shabelle rivers.

CONFLICT AMONG THE CLANS

Somalis believe that the first tribal systems to develop, after the Samaale tribe, were the Irir and the Darod clans. The Irir clan then divided into the northern clans of the Dir, the Isaq, and the Hawiye.

The two major agricultural clans to split from the Samaale tribe were the Digil and the Rahanwayn, who settled in the south.

This division into six distinct clans of north and south came about as early Somali tribes roamed the country in search of water and pasture for their livestock. As they had to fight each other for land, pasture, and water, they began to split up into further sub-clans.

The clans also fought over religion and trade. Different environments and conflicts caused the clans to evolve differently. The pastoral or nomadic clans lived in the desert and low-brush regions suitable for raising camels, sheep, and goats, while the agricultural clans settled in the areas between the main rivers, choosing to cultivate the land and raise cattle. The nomadic tribes soon began to consider themselves superior, and to this day, they are held in high regard by the general population.

Since the demise of Socialism, and because of the lack of a central government, the clans have become a powerful force in the country, both politically and socially. Today, hardly a single area is left in the average Somali's life that is not controlled by one clan or another.

A gunman protecting a crop of corn in the town of Marka, in case of a raid by an opposing clan.

50

OUTSIDER CLANS WITH A SECRET LANGUAGE

Somalis historically regarded the pastoral nomads as the elite members of society, while the agricultural tribes were seen as the "middle class." Both these groups in turn looked on all outsiders as the "lower class." Certain occupations such as hunting, forging, and leather-tanning were traditionally performed by Somali people of various ethnic origins. These people, who looked and spoke like Somalis, then formed their own "clans," or occupational groups.

Some historians believe that members of these occupational clans were really Somalis by origin who had been ostracized from society because of the work they do.

Many of the so-called lower classes have lineages similar to those of the existing Somali clans. But because these groups often spoke a "secret" language (actually, nothing more than slang), the Somalis have regarded them as a people of unknown ethnic origins.

The pastoral clans call these groups the Sab, meaning "low," and the agricultural clans refer to them as "low caste." They make up about 1% of the Somali population.

Many of them, about 75% of the total, work as barbers, circumcisers, and hunters. This large group call themselves the Midgaan. The other 25%, the Tumaal, work primarily with metal.

Despite their lowly status in Somali society, certain members of the occupational groups are consulted by the upper and middle classes, who believe them to have magical powers. They are hired on special occasions—to bless a Somali wedding, baptize a baby, or act as fortune tellers.

PRIDE IN CRAFTWORK

This Somali craftsman uses an L-shaped tool for his work.

Since the time of the earliest settlers, Somalis have shown a talent for craftwork. They make sure the tools they use fit their hands well. To them, their tools are an extension of their arms and they take pride in making and maintaining these tools.

Once crafted, an object may serve the owner for many years. This is especially true of the shepherd's stick, which the nomads carry with them wherever they go.

Commonly represented in Somali craftwork is the symbol of four triangles or a large triangle with smaller triangles within it. The four triangles indicate the four corners of the world and the large triangle symbolizes the eye of God. Often represented are other religious symbols such as the journey to Mecca and the life of the Prophet Mohammed.

Village craftsmen used to pass on their skills to their male children, but this tradition has been eroded over the years as more Somalis are moving into the towns and cities. In certain villages, good examples of stone work, pottery, rugs, leatherwork, and jewelry can still be found.

WAYS OF DRESSING

Somalia's hot dry climate dictates what people wear. In rural areas, nomadic men usually wear a long white cloth that is wound around the waist and draped over the shoulders.

For many men, hair is an important feature of their appearance. While many have standard haircuts, some of the men cover their heads with women's hair and with mud. Others use henna to dye their hair red. Often, the men apply butter to their hair as an insecticide.

Rural Somali women also wear a long cloth, called a *guntina* ("goon-TEE-nah"), that they wind around their bodies and tie in a knot on their right shoulder. Unlike the piece of cloth worn by the men, the *guntina* is made of beautiful, colorful material that the women purchase in small stores.

Married women usually tie their hair back with a black scarf and wear another long flowing scarf over their head and arms.

In the cities, Somali businessmen wear casual suits to work. The women tend to wear dresses. They may buy a length of bright material meant for the *guntina*, but get it tailor-made into a traditional or modern dress. Because of Western influence in the country over the years, the European style of dressing is preferred in cities. These days, even rural women may choose flowing dresses of flowered cotton or embroidery, rather than the *guntina*.

A city woman wearing a Western-style dress made from a *guntina* length of cloth.

LIFESTYLE

THE NOMADS OF SOMALIA share a way of life that is governed by the ruthless Somali desert. They roam the land, moving families and herds in the vast countryside, toward the next pasture. This nomadic lifestyle has remained unchanged for thousands of years.

It took the severe droughts of the 1970s and 1980s to bring many nomads to the refugee camps. They had no choice then but to give up their wandering life, as they and their animals were dying of thirst and starvation in the desert. As soon as the famines ended, the nomads that survived left the camps once more for the scattered pastures.

Family and clan play a highly important role in the lives of the nomads. This is more so for the wandering nomads than for those already settled into a semi-agricultural community. Nomads belong to one of the four pastoral tribal clans. Because of the size of these clans, close associations are formed within each group, forming a sub-clan of between four and eight people.

Members of these smaller groups are extremely supportive of one another. Traditionally, when one member of a sub-clan commits an injustice against a member of another sub-clan, the two groups will attempt to mediate by exchanging camels. If the matter is not resolved, violence may erupt, with the sub-clans defending their own group vigorously.

Opposite: **A field worker, striking in bright clothes and carrying leather water pitchers.**

Below: **Two nomads load their donkey in preparation for the long trek ahead.**

THE SOMALI'S TRUE COUSIN

When a Somali refers to a brother or sister, this term can include distant relatives as well as actual siblings. A Somali's "true cousin" can be someone separated by two generations. Three generations separate second cousins, and third cousins are separated by four generations.

Three generations of Somalis outside their house.

Although the Somali people trace their roots patrilineally, that is, through the male side of the family, the mother plays a central role.

Divorce is common in Somali society, and a woman will often marry several men during her lifetime and bear children by each of them. Therefore, children of different fathers often live with their mother after the fathers have left, or remarried, or chosen to live with one of their other wives.

Child care is the woman's responsibility, and she will usually not want a former husband's new wife to look after her children. For this reason, a child's closest ties are often forged with maternal relatives, despite the patrilineal nature of Somali society.

Although a child is not obligated to maternal relatives, who do not bear ultimate responsibility for him or her, a child quite often consults or appeals to these relatives when in need or in trouble.

CHAIN OF LOYALTY

Somalis faithfully observe a chain of loyalty—family, lineage, sub-clan, clan or tribe, and nation. A popular saying in Somalia and in Arab nations summarizes this succinctly, "I against my brother; I and my brother against my cousin; I, my brother, and my cousin against the world." There is an exception to this rule. Because of the country's liberal views on divorce and bigamy, families tend to be very large. Sometimes, brothers and sisters with a common mother find themselves ranged on opposing sides, usually due to disagreements between their fathers. As their ultimate allegiance is toward their own father, bitter conflict between half-siblings can result.

Somali children learn from a very young age to value an honorable reputation and to avoid harming the family or clan name. As Muslims, Somalis hold views on life that are greatly influenced by their religion. They believe, for instance, that fate controls their lives.

Most Somalis are convinced that men and women are not equal but are actually very different in both nature and social status. Somalis also hold the elderly in high regard, believing that wisdom increases with age.

This group of people are all variously related to each other.

SOMALIS' VIEW OF STRANGERS

Somalis are loyal and generous people who honor and support their family and friends. But they do not give the same consideration to strangers, which often offends foreigners. Somalis particularly distrust white people, a hangover from the days of colonial rule.

Some Somalis socialize with white people, but there are those who continue to resent them and regard them as impure people. In general, after Somalis have made friends with a foreigner, they will be quite accommodating. Travelers who cannot find a place to stay may be invited into a Somali home for the night.

Not that there are many foreign travelers in the country. Due to past Soviet influence, civil wars, and famines, Somalia is not a popular tourist spot. The Somalis are therefore unaccustomed to foreigners, and it takes them a little time to warm up to visitors.

MARRIAGES AND GIFTS

Traditionally, a Somali man decided whom he would marry and arranged all details with the father of the bride. This system of arranged marriages often led to older men paying a lot of money to the fathers of young girls in exchange for a marriage agreement. Today the younger generation of Somalis tend to select a spouse based on typical marriage values such as love, honor, and respect.

Whether the marriage is arranged or not, the groom's family presents a gift of camel, or cattle, or money to the bride's family. This gift is given serious consideration because it represents the level of esteem toward the bride and her family. After the wedding, it is the bride's family who may have to present the young couple with a home. A marriage is seen not just as a relationship between two people, but also as a link between two separate families.

Most Somalis marry outside of their primary lineage, and the woman will leave her family or clan to live with her husband. Women, as a mark of loyalty to their own family, retain their family name on marriage rather than assume their husband's name.

Two men driving their cattle home. A head of cattle is a welcome wedding gift for the bride's family.

During the marriage ceremony, which has to take place before a sheikh, the couple sign legal documents that stipulate how much money the man has to give his wife if they divorce. The settlement consists of money, animals, land, or jewelry, and immediately becomes the wife's personal property. Until the couple divorces, the husband keeps the property in trust. If it is the wife and not the husband who wants a divorce, the woman usually has to give up her right to this property.

A MAN MAY HAVE FOUR WIVES

Under Islamic law, polygamy is accepted and condoned—but only for men. A man may have as many as four wives at one time, if he can support them equally. Because of this, the children of each wife often become very protective of their mother, knowing that she has to compete with the other wives for their father's love and attention.

A Somali household may commonly consist of one husband, four wives, and many children. In such a case, most wives prefer to live in a separate dwelling from their husband, rather than share the same roof with another woman. The husband usually spends some time in rotation between the homes of his different wives.

A woman and her four children. Children of divorced parents usually choose to stay with the mother.

DIVORCE, SOMALI STYLE

If a man wants a divorce, all he has to do is repeat three times to his wife, "I divorce you." Once the couple is divorced, there is still a three-month waiting period, to make sure the wife is not pregnant.

If a woman wants to remarry an ex-husband, she must first marry and divorce another man. This problem does not arise too often, because couples usually divorce when the wife is too old to bear children, so the men are more likely to marry a younger woman than remarry a former spouse.

STILL A LONG WAY TO GO FOR SOMALI WOMEN

Somalia remains a male-dominated society, but women have gained more freedom since 1969. Muslim law allows women to own, inherit, and pass on property. Somali women have also become more educated over the past 25 years, and some are now aspiring to career positions that used to be held only by men.

On the whole, Somali society still expects women to be submissive toward men and to be well-behaved under all circumstances. Young women may advance only by exercising self-restraint, obeying and deferring to men, and displaying an attitude of self-denial. A striking example of how women are treated as inferior is the cruel tradition of "circumcising" young girls. This practice has been more accurately described as female genital mutilation (FGM) by the United Nations. It originated as a way to keep young women pure until marriage.

Modern Muslim leaders shun the practice of FGM and have ordered its followers to discontinue this barbaric act. Nonetheless, over 98% of Somali women have been made to undergo FGM. Even those Somali men who abhor this practice make their daughters go through the ordeal because they are afraid that if they do not, no worthy man will want to marry their daughters.

Two Somali girls bring home the firewood.

SOMALI CHILDREN

Due to the nature of close-knit families and clans, children are a very visible part of Somali society. Somali parents love and cherish their children, but bring them up with strict discipline and punish them for misbehaving or for dishonoring the family name.

Because divorce is so common in Somalia, children often live with only one of their parents, usually the mother. Sometimes boys will live with the father and his new wife rather than with the mother, perhaps owing to reasons of clan loyalty. In this case, the boy is welcomed by the father and his new family into the household.

Somali children grow up with many other children—siblings, cousins, and step-siblings. The adults in their life include not just the parents, but also step-parents, grandparents, aunts, uncles, and sometimes great-grandparents.

Children are the means of bonding between different families and clans. Until a married woman bears a child, her loyalty remains more with her own family and clan. After the child is born, the wife gives her loyalty to her husband, and even her relatives may develop a strong sense of connection to her husband and his family.

IMAN: THE RETURN OF THE NATIVE

One of the world's most well-known fashion models of the 1970s and 1980s is a Somali woman called Iman. Apart from pursuing an international modeling career, she is also a Hollywood actress and married to the British rock star David Bowie.

Iman was born in the capital city of Mogadishu in 1955 to well-off, educated parents. Her father was an ambassador for Somalia and her mother was a nurse. When Siad Barre took power in 1969, he arrested all civilian politicians. Iman's father was placed under house arrest but he and his family later sought political asylum in Tanzania.

Iman lived in Mogadishu until she was 17 years old, when she went to university in Nairobi in Kenya. One day she was spotted by a Western photographer on a Nairobi street. The next thing she knew, she was hailed as the fashion world's next supermodel. When she was flown to New York, 64 photographers greeted her at the airport. The West was intrigued by Iman's beauty and heritage, although she was also described as a sheep-herder, in spite of being well-educated and speaking five languages.

In 1992, after an absence of 25 years, Iman returned to her native land for a visit. She was reunited with her family and visited the refugee camps, where she was shocked by the death and destruction. She then made a documentary—about a land ravaged and desolate from famines and civil wars. Iman's trip proved enlightening both to her and to the viewers of her moving documentary.

Somalis are a good-looking people. They are generally tall and slim with attractive features and fine skin.

GETTING BETTER EDUCATED

The Somali educational system has improved a great deal over the past 30 years, with emphasis being placed on the education of children. Despite this, the illiteracy rate remained around 85% until the early 1990s. One incident in the civil wars contributed to this. In the general mayhem of the civil war of 1992, people forced their way into the national teacher-training center in Mogadishu and stole the desks. The school was shut down and became a refugee camp, which led to a shortage of trained teachers.

In 1993, Somalia reopened the school to over 200 children between the ages of 6 and 12. The International Islamic Relief Organization provided enough money to Somalia in 1993 to open 19 schools. Most of the schools segregate pupils by sex until university level. Pupils in the primary grades learn reading, writing, languages, and mathematics. After primary school, students attend secondary schools or vocational schools to learn skills in industry, agriculture, and commerce.

The Somali National University was founded in 1971. Courses available include law, education, economics, agriculture, science, veterinary science, engineering, economics, medicine, and geology. About 4,000 Somalis attend the university, and more women are enrolled today than in the past.

Children in class. Most pupils are segregated by sex until they reach university level.

RAVAGED CITIES

Over the past decade, Somalia's cities have been ravaged by civil wars. Many areas of Mogadishu, for instance, have been reduced to ruins. The civil wars between north and south have brought poverty to the urban areas, as well as a population imbalance.

Wealthy residents of the cities have fled to other countries, while those whose lives have been disrupted by the civil wars in the rural areas have been moving steadily into the cities.

Today, Somalis are returning to the big towns and cities to rebuild their homes and offices, and to try and get on with life as best they can. The most basic Somali home is the *arish* ("AH-reesh"), a rectangular building with timber, straw, dung, and mud walls and a pitched tin or thatched roof.

An improvement on the *arish* is the *baraca* ("bah-RAH-kah"), which is rectangular with cement floors and timber walls. If it has stone or cement walls, the Somalis call it a *casa matoni* ("KAH-sa ma-TOH-nee").

Two other styles of Somali homes resemble those in the West. The *casa moro* ("KAH-sah MOH-roh") is a two-story house built in stone, in the Arabic style. The best houses in the cities are those built in the European style, with pitched tile roofs, walled courtyards, and stone walls.

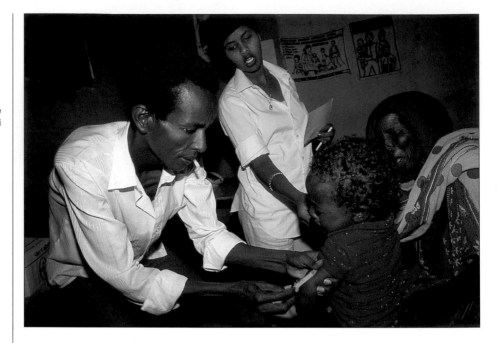

HEALTH AND WELFARE

Although many aspects of Somali life improved after independence in 1960, the health and the welfare of the citizens significantly declined, mainly because of famine, droughts, warfare, and floods. The government also failed to set up an acceptable health care system for its citizens. The fall of Socialism brought about a further decline. In the 1990s, doctors and hospital beds were in grave shortage.

One of the most common diseases in Somalia is tuberculosis. This affects many young men who are camel herders. Because of their harsh life and working conditions, they contract the disease from their camels and then transmit it to others as they travel. The cities have been more successful in curbing tuberculosis than the smaller towns, as more nomads pass through the towns.

More than half the population suffers from malaria or sickness caused by internal parasites. While neither of these is immediately fatal, their victims become weak and susceptible to other diseases. But malnutrition is probably the most deadly scourge of all in Somalia. Droughts and famines have taken the lives of thousands of Somalis over the past decade.

There was only one doctor to every 10,000 Somalis in the early 1990s.

MOVING HOUSE

Many rural Somalis live in makeshift homes or one-story houses with thatched roofs and dirt floors. The traditional rural home of the nomadic Somali tribes is a domed hut called an *akal* ("ah-KAHL"), which is made from pliable sticks tied together at the top and covered by a domed covering of hide or matting. Some nomads make these homes waterproof by weaving the matting on top very tightly. In small towns, the huts are covered with cardboard, cloth, and flattened tin.

The nomads can erect and dismantle these homes in about two hours. Usually the women take down the *akals,* while the men begin the search for new pastures. The women also make utensils, weave ropes, fetch firewood, load and unload the camels with every move, care for the family's herd, and process the livestock products.

The *akals*, traditional homes of the nomadic and agricultural Somalis.

The nomads never reside in towns or cities. They pitch their tents or domed huts near pastures and water needed by their herds. Once the water dries up, they take down their homes, load their belongings on their backs, and move on to the next spot.

The homes in small rural towns are not so easily dismantled, as their owners do not move as often as the nomads. A Somali's day in the countryside begins very early, usually with the milking of cows.

RELIGION

RELIGION IS ONE OF THE most important aspects of a Somali's life. The state religion is Islam and most Somalis practice this faith. There is also a small Christian population in the country.

Somalia is a member of the Arab League, a group of Arab Muslim states that have banded together to conform politically and religiously with other Muslims. Membership in the Arab League was considered prudent because most of Somalia's African neighbors follow the Christian faith or indigenous African religions.

Islam has an overwhelming influence on everyday life. Schools teach the religion, which in turn dictates marriage and divorce laws. Nearly all Muslims in Somalia are Sunnis, who follow the Sufi school of Islam and believe that their religious leaders should be elected by the people.

The other sect of Muslims, the Shiites, split with the Sunnis after the death of the Prophet Mohammed. The Shiites believe that only the descendants of Mohammed should become religious leaders, claiming that these men possess superior powers.

Somali Muslims, although following the same beliefs as other Muslims, have modified Islam to their particular heritage. For instance, contrary to other Sunnis, Somalis believe that their leaders possess the power to bless and curse individuals. They call this *baruka* ("bah-ROO-kah") and believe it to be a God-given power entrusted to both religious and secular leaders.

Opposite: **Somalis inside a mosque. Some are reading the Koran.**

Below: **This mosque in Mogadishu was built with the help of the Kuwaiti government.**

HOLY MEN WHO BECOME SAINTS

In addition to worshiping Allah and Mohammed, the Muslim Somalis also venerate their saints. The tombs of Muslim saints are to be found all over the country. Often, the holy men of Somalia become saints after they die.

A holy man is someone who owns no property or goods and has given up everything to go about preaching the word of Allah. He earns the title of saint upon his death, if he is deemed to have been deeply spiritual and have performed acts of kindness and mercy to those in need.

The widow of a man declared a saint has to build a small mosque over his burial site and care for his grave. Somali Muslims believe that the power of a saint is at its strongest during the month of his death. At such a time, believers gather at his grave to pray and to listen to verses from the Koran. These visitors often tear a remnant from their clothes, tie the cloth around the railing of the tomb, and promise to perform a good deed if the saint grants their wish.

Muslims learn that the Prophet Mohammed was visited by an angel who gave him God's words in Arabic, which eventually became the Koran.

FIVE PILLARS OF ISLAM

The Prophet Mohammed, who taught and spread the religion of Islam, was born around A.D. 571 during a time of civil unrest. He heard the voice of God or Allah urging him to "cry in the name of thy Lord."

When Mohammed told his wife of this experience, she became his first convert. Over the years of his life, Mohammed converted thousands of people to Islam, and by the time he died, almost everyone in the Arab world had embraced the faith.

All over the world, Muslims follow strict principles called the Five Pillars of Islam. The first pillar is the *shahada* ("sha-HAH-dah"), a creed that every Muslim must proclaim. The *shahada* states: "There is no God but Allah, and Mohammed is His Prophet."

The second pillar requires Muslims to pray five times a day, each time facing the holy city of Mecca in Saudi Arabia. Muslims need not go to a mosque to pray but may pray wherever they happen to be. Many Somali Muslims therefore carry a prayer mat with them to use for their five daily prayer sessions.

Zakat ("ZAH-kaht"), or giving to those less fortunate, is the third pillar of Islam. The fourth pillar is to observe the holy month of Ramadan, during which Muslims must fast from dawn to dusk. The fifth pillar of Islam is the mandatory pilgrimage to Mecca.

THE KORAN

The Muslim holy book is called the Koran. Most of the principles of the Christian Bible are also found in this Islamic holy book. And because Judaism follows the Old Testament, the three religions are closely related.

Muslims believe that their religion is one complete faith created through the continuation of the beliefs of Christianity and Judaism. The Koran, like the Bible, teaches that both Heaven and Hell exist. Both the holy books stress a belief in God, and both relate the story of the creation of humankind in the Garden of Eden.

In the Koran, Muslims, Jews, and Christians are all regarded as "children of the book."

ROMAN CATHOLIC CATHEDRAL

During the time of colonial rule and when Italian influence was at its height in the country, the Italians built a Roman Catholic cathedral in Mogadishu, which is one of the few Christian places of worship in the country. Just next door to this cathedral is a mosque.

In fact, mosques can be found all over Somalia, especially in the larger cities. Some of them are architecturally beautiful. In Mogadishu, local residents believe that the Sheikh Abdul Aziz mosque, with its distinctive round minaret, emerged from the sea. Outside the cities, there are smaller mosques, as well as the remains of ancient mosques.

A priest stands on the balcony of the Roman Catholic cathedral in Mogadishu.

TEN RITES FOR PILGRIMS TO PERFORM IN MECCA

Mecca, the birthplace of the Prophet Mohammed, is in the Hejaz province of Saudi Arabia. Certain strict rules have to be observed when making the pilgrimage to this holy city. Muslims always arrive in Mecca on foot. Those who live too far away may need to take a plane to Saudi Arabia and continue the rest of the journey on foot.

When pilgrims are about six miles (10 km) away from Mecca, they divide into separate groups of the same sex. They then bathe in a special fluid and put on appropriate clothes.

Once they arrive in Mecca, they must perform 10 rites in a specific order. First they enter the Gate of Peace to the city. Second they kiss the black stone of the Ka'bah, a cube-shaped monument in the Grand Mosque of Mecca. After that they circle the Ka'bah seven times, touching the black stone on each of their seven rounds. Then they stop to pray at the tomb of Abraham. Next they climb to the tops of Mount Marwah and Mount Safa and run between the two mountains seven times.

The sixth rite involves a journey to Mount Arafat. Once at Arafat, they fulfill the seventh rite by listening to a sermon. The eighth rite is a celebration in the city of Muzdalifah, which lies between Mecca and Mount Arafat. Next the Muslims use special stones to throw at the pillars in Mina, signifying that they are stoning the "devils." The final rite is a visit to the tomb of Mohammed. After going to the tomb and honoring Allah's prophet, the journey is complete.

THE POWER OF PRAYER

There is a well-known tale among Somalis of the half-blind saint, Sheikh Ali Gure. He was once traveling with three attendants when he asked them to leave him alone for a few hours. After some time his attendants returned to the spot where they had left him sitting on the ground, but he was not there and they could not find him.

Eventually the sheikh materialized at the same spot and told his attendants a wondrous story. It appeared that Muslims at sea were in trouble because their boat had sustained damage. They prayed to Allah to mend their boat, and through Allah's power, Sheikh Gure was sent to them. He was able to place a board over the hole in their boat, making it watertight. Then by that same power, he returned to his original spot on the ground.

FAMOUS SOMALI SAINTS

Both adults and children are familiar with the names of their saints. Children are told about these saints through the village storyteller or learn about them in school.

Children being given religious instruction.

The most famous Somali saint is Sheikh Muhr Mohammed from Hargeysa, who wrote religious poetry in Arabic and translated traditional hymns from Arabic to Somali. During a severe drought, the Somalis asked Sheikh Mohammed to pray for rain. Within a couple of hours, rain fell on the region and saved the crops and animals.

Two other famous Somali saints are Sheikh Abd ar Rahman Abdullah and Sheikh Ali Maye. Sheikh Abdullah had a reputation for sanctity and the gift of prophecy. Today his followers still circulate his writings and visit his tomb in Mogadishu. Of the saint Sheikh Ali Maye, it is told that one day he met a young boy who could not speak or read. The saint then slapped the boy on the head, and the boy began to speak and read fluent Arabic.

SUNNI MUSLIM SECTS

Most Somalis are Sunnis who follow the Sufi school of belief. Within the Sufi school are three divisions—the Qadiriya, the Salihiya, and the Ahmediya. The Qadiriya is the oldest sect of Islam and was founded in Baghdad in 1166. Somalis became associated with this sect in 1883.

The first Qadiriya leader in Somalia was Sheikh Abdarahman al Zeilawi, who preached the faith in the northern regions and in Ethiopia. Different leaders introduced the Qadiriya sect to the southern regions of Somalia at about the same time. The Qadiriya are considered highly spiritual people because they remove themselves from modern problems.

Muhammad ibn Salih founded the Salihiya sect in 1887 in Ethiopia. Within a couple of years, this sect was gaining followers in Somalia. Along the Shabelle River, a man named Sheikh Muhammad Guled ar Rashidi became a regional leader of the Salihiya sect. The Salihiyas are regarded as the most fanatic sect of Sunni Muslims.

The third group of Somali Sunnis, the Ahmediya, was founded by Sayyid Ahmad ibn Idris al Fasi of Mecca. The faith was brought to Somalia at the end of the 19th century by Sheikh Ali Maye. The Ahmediyas have rituals of simple prayers and hymns, during which followers fall into a trance. Ahmediyan leaders concentrate on teaching the Koran and the Hadith, which is a book of legends about the Prophet Mohammed.

75

PRAYERS AND POLITICS

Religion has always played an important role in the governing of Somalia. After independence in 1960, Somalis were granted the right of freedom of religion, but at the same time Islam was declared the state religion.

When the Socialists came to power in 1969, they published a paper discussing the role of Islam in the new government and distinguishing between scientific and Islamic Socialism. Islamic Socialism was deemed

During the years of Communist and Socialist rule, the government tried to impose its own brand of "religion" on the population, one that it called scientific Socialism.

EVIL SPIRITS IN FOLK BELIEFS

In Somalia, as in many other African nations, folklore is an inseparable part of religion. For example, Somalis believe that someone may give them the "evil eye," which causes a bad spirit to enter their soul. The victim may suffer sneezing, coughing, vomiting, or red bumps on the skin. The cure for this would be for a religious leader to hold a ceremony in which he reads the Koran to the sufferer, makes him drink water, and bathes him in perfume.

Another belief among Somalis is possession by an evil spirit called the *zar* ("zahr"). The victims are always women who have grievances against their husbands, and the symptoms are fainting and hysteria. If a woman is possessed by this evil spirit, her community holds a religious ceremony to exorcise the spirit.

A third type of spirit is called the *gelid* ("GAY-lid"). A person so possessed usually has injured another person, and so the remedy for this is also a ceremony consisting of readings from the Koran.

It is also believed that people who are poor, helpless, or injured are protected by Allah, who gives them special powers that they may use to help others. Such powers can also be used to hurt others. As a result, Somalis believe that they have to be kind to someone less fortunate, or else that person will place an evil spell on them.

LONG MOURNING PERIOD FOR SOMALI WIDOWS

When a Somali woman's husband dies, she must adhere to a strict Muslim ritual after his death. She must remain in mourning for four months and 10 days. During this time, Islam dictates that she must wear only white clothes and remain at home. She cannot touch grease or a man's hand, and she can only shower and wash her hair once or twice a week. The widow must save all of the hairs from her comb and keep her nail clippings.

At the end of the mourning period, several sheikhs and two or three religious women arrive at the widow's home. The women take the widow into the bathroom where they wash her hair and body and dress her in new clothes of the widow's favorite color.

Once the widow is clean and in her new clothes, everyone, including the sheikhs, go outside the house to bury her hair combings and nail clippings. The sheikhs then pray for the widow and her dead husband. After they have read out parts of the Koran, the ceremony ends, and everyone celebrates the end of the mourning.

to favor capitalism and the richer class. Scientific Socialism, on the other hand, was supposed to have the same values as Islam itself and did not discriminate between people by class or wealth.

When many religious leaders rebelled against the ideas of the new regime, the Socialists arrested them, accusing them of anti-Islamic and anti-government activities. During the 1970s, religious and government leaders continued to disagree on the role of Islam in government. In 1975 President Barre gave women a number of new rights, including the right to inherit equally with men, and he credited the Koran for his decision. But religious leaders protested strongly against the new law.

The government's answer was ruthless. Ten religious leaders from Mogadishu were executed. After the execution, other religious chiefs kept a low profile, but they resumed their secular role in Somali society when the Socialist government collapsed in 1991. Today the Muslim sects and the clans have great power and virtually rule the country.

President Siad Barre introduced many rights for Somali women, but this was seen as an attempt to undermine the basic structure of Islamic society.

LANGUAGE

MANY SOMALIS ARE FLUENT in five or more languages. Because the Koran is written in Arabic, all Somali Muslims are familiar with this language. Some Somalis also speak French, Italian, or English because of past colonial rule. But the official language is Somali, which belongs to a linguistic group called lowland Eastern Cushitic. It is also related to languages in Ethiopia, Djibouti, and Kenya.

Although the written form of Somali was introduced only since 1972, the spoken form has been used for centuries. The Somali tongue resembles languages spoken in nearby African countries. Even during British and Italian control of Somalia, the people continued to speak Somali while learning the colonial languages.

The Somali tongue has several dialects that vary according to region. The most widely used of these is Common Somali, while the others are Coastal and Central Somali.

Until 1972, English and Italian were the two official languages of the government. Somalis who spoke either English or Italian therefore had better career opportunities in government and business circles.

When the Somali script was finally established in 1972, the government required all of its officials to learn it. Attempts too were made to teach urban and rural Somalis how to read and write the language. These attempts were not too successful, as the country still has a high illiteracy rate.

Opposite: **A boy holds up a writing tablet inscribed with Arabic script.**

Below: **The doorway of a bookshop in Mogadishu.**

79

THE SACRED TONGUE

Most Somalis are fluent in Arabic, or at least understand it. Arabic is the sixth official language of the United Nations and is the sacred tongue of the Muslims. It originated in Saudi Arabia during the seventh century, but was not recorded in writing until many centuries later.

Arabic is difficult to learn, as it is very different from most other languages. Somalis, like other Muslims, consider Arabic to be Allah's (God's) language. There are three tongues in Arabic; the one known to Somalis is classical Arabic, the language of the Koran.

Arabic script, with its beautiful and artistic calligraphy, looks very different from the script of most modern languages. When the government was deciding on a written form of Somali, many religious leaders were disappointed that the form eventually picked resembled English rather than the Arabic script.

Somali children off to school. They learn to read and write at least two languages.

NAMES

Somalis have long names that tell a lot about their lineage. When a child is born, the parents give him or her a personal name.

After this, the names given are the child's father's personal name, the personal name of the father's father, and so on, up to the name of the founder of the sub-clan, and then finally, the name of the clan family.

People in the same families and clans tend to live near each other in the cities and towns. When a Somali visits a strange town, he or she can always track down relatives or

SOMALI WORDS

Many Somali words have Arabic origins. Over 90% of Somalis are Muslims, but their language is quite different from Arabic and even has regional variations. The difference between Common Somali and the other tongues is somewhat similar to that between Spanish and Portuguese. As in these European languages, the words in the Somali tongues have basically the same roots but are pronounced differently according to region. Words may also have a different prefix or suffix.

Some of the most widely used Common Somali words are:

English Meaning	Somali Word	English Meaning	Somali Word
One	Kow	Yes	Ha
Two	Laba	No	Maya
Three	Sader	Food	Ahnto
Four	Afar	Bread	Roti
Five	Shan	Rice	Baris
Ten	Toban	Meat	Hillip
Hundred	Bogol	Water	Beeyu
Thousand	Kuhn	Tea	Shah
Good morning	Subah wanaqsan	Where is?	Hage?
Good afternoon	Galeb wanaqsan	How much?	Waa imissa?
Good evening	Habeen wanaqsan	Toilet	Musghul

clan family simply by asking where a certain "name" can be found. Families always welcome their relatives into their home, even if they have never seen them before.

Not only is a person's name helpful for locating hospitable relatives, it tells a Somali how closely he or she is related to others simply by comparing the orders of the names. The more names they have in common, the more closely they are related. For instance, brothers and sisters have the same names except for their first or personal names. Cousins have different first and second names, and these are their personal names and their fathers' personal names. But their other names will be the same.

People who are related only through the clan family have different names except for the very last name. Because their names are so long, Somalis rarely use their full names.

WORD PLAY AND HUMOR

As a country without a written language until 1972, Somalis have relied on their memory and verbal skills to recount history and tell important news. People earned the respect of others by mastering such skills.

Somali society has always judged those in power, such as political or religious leaders, by their ability to use the Somali language to full advantage. These leaders are expected to use ornamental speech by means of poetry, vivid words, and alliteration.

Negotiating is a delicate skill in Somalia because Somalis do not like to be blunt in a request for a favor, or to receive a blunt refusal. So before asking another to perform a task or cooperate on a project, a Somali will approach the subject indirectly, to discover the other person's general attitude. If the person responds favorably, then the Somali will state his request. If the response is unfavorable, the embarrassment of a refusal has been avoided.

The use of humor is another important communication skill in everyday language. Somalis, like people of other nations, use humor quite often to remove themselves from awkward situations.

A person who is just learning the language would probably be lost without a full understanding of the way Somalis use humorous word play.

This man is displaying a placard written in both English and Somali, stating the aim of his group, the United Somalia Salvation Youth.

MANNERS OF GREETING

When Somalis meet each other, the men always shake hands. A woman usually waits until a man extends his hand before offering her own. Usually men and women will not have any physical contact when meeting, unless they happen to be members of the same family.

When greeting each other, families hug and kiss, as people do in other countries. Members of the same sex often embrace, or they kiss each other on the cheek.

A group of women in town have a chat before the morning marketing.

NONVERBAL BEHAVIOR AND GESTURES

Although Somalia is an African nation, its religious and cultural alliances have always been with the Arab nations. Most Somalis know Arabic well enough to recite the Koran from memory.

Even nonverbal communication in Somalia has been influenced by that of the Arab nations. The following are universal Arabic gestures, used by Arabs and Somalis alike:

1. Moving the right hand up and down with the palm facing down means "Be quiet."
2. Holding the right hand out while opening and closing the hand means "Come here."
3. Moving the right hand away from the body with the palm facing down means "Go away."
4. Placing the right hand on the heart after shaking hands signifies sincerity.
5. Raising the eyebrows with a tilted-back head, or shaking the right forefinger from right to left means "No."

ARTS

SOMALIA HAS A RICH CULTURAL HISTORY, going back to ancient Egyptian times. The Egyptian influence began when Queen Hatshepsut of Egypt sent men to Somalia, then known as the Land of Punt, to obtain incense, ivory, skins, and spices. By the seventh century, Arab and Persian traders were also making their presence felt.

By the 10th century, Arab and Persian influences were reflected in Somali artwork such as swords, daggers, marble objects, and pottery. Examples of such objects can be seen today in the museums of the big cities. Fine examples of craftwork, including jewelry, woven mats, and drums made from skins and tree fibers, are also on display.

The Somalis did not have a written form of poetry until recently, but their skills of verbal poetry are well practiced and they have passed down their poems through the generations.

Left: **A woman drummer performing during a holiday celebration.**

Opposite: **Somali women are skilled at weaving intricate mats or rugs from natural fibers.**

Arabic script taken from the Koran: "The sun never eclipses the sky."

ISLAM ON SOMALI ART

Islam has been the most significant influence on Somali art over the centuries. Because most Somali artists were Muslims, their art reflected their religious beliefs. Scenes from the Koran were often depicted, or religious symbols were included in an otherwise secular painting.

It was only during the 1970s and 1980s that the Islamic influence was absent from works of art. This was because the Socialist regime had ordered artists to incorporate socialist propaganda into their work instead.

Islam forbids the portrayal of humans or animals in art, so artistic subjects tend to be flowers, vases, or creatures of the imagination. Colors are bright and vibrant, a favorite being "Mohammed Blue"—a color that the ancient Chinese developed in honor of the Prophet.

Islamic art is rich with intricate designs, and these often appear on paintings, pottery, ceramics, tiles, and carpets. Some Muslim artists design wall hangings for private homes, incorporating verses from the Koran. Because the Arabic script is so beautiful, such wall hangings are very attractive and often look like works of art.

ALL THE WORLD'S A STAGE

Most works of drama performed in Somalia before the 1950s originated in other countries, but for the last 40 years or so, Somalis have been writing their own plays. Somalis are natural performers and have produced their own plays at the National Theater in Mogadishu or at theaters in other cities.

Drama was part of the school curriculum in British Somaliland, with an emphasis on taking part in school plays. From that, Somalis graduated to producing plays in town halls and to writing their own plays. In Italian Somaliland, the Italians too helped Somalis write and produce their own plays.

When the nation obtained a written Somali script, plays began to be written in Somali, as well as in English and Italian. Today playwrights write in Somali, Arabic, English, and Italian. One of Somali's foremost dramatists is Hassan Mumin, who is also a poet and broadcaster.

A crowd at a holiday celebration applauds a performer giving a one-man show.

SO MUCH MORE EXPRESSIVE TO USE CAMEL TALK

Camels are so vital to the Somalis that they have caused rivalry and feuds between communities and clans. As such, the animal has a special place in the literary tradition of the country. Poets use what are known as "camel metaphors" to express feelings of love, hate, jealousy, and desire.

Even ordinary Somalis have a repertoire of "camel expressions" reflecting the importance of the camel in their daily lives. For instance, there is an area in Somalia called *Candho-qoy* ("KAHN-doh-koy"), meaning "the place of moist udders," while another word, *geel-weyta* ("GEEL-WEY-tah"), means "the place that weakens animals." Scholars call their research *raadra* ("RAAH-drah"), literally "to trace lost animals." Problems set out in a school textbook are called *layis* ("LAH-yis"), which refers to the "breaking of a young camel."

ART OF STORYTELLING

Storytelling is a traditional art in Somalia. From one generation to the next, those who cannot read or write but have a gift for storytelling are able to pass on true or fictional anecdotes of value. One well-known Somali story, of a man called Gurgati and his two sons, tells why there came to be two classes of people in Somalia.

Gurgati lived in the countryside with his family. When the land was hit by drought, Gurgati asked his two older sons to go and find water for their goats, sheep, camels, and cows. The sons, who had never been on such a mission before, asked Gurgati what they should do if they could not find water and wandered too far away from home.

Gurgati's reply was that they should continue until they found water, no matter how far from home that took them. They must walk in the morning, but stop to rest when it got hot, then continue walking in the evening. Gurgati warned them that if they saw a dead animal or anything else they could eat, they should eat only enough to keep them alive and not fill their stomach or take the meat with them.

When they found food and water, Gurgati added, they should then vomit up everything they had eaten, because the animal carcass they had eaten had not been freshly killed. And they should then wash themselves. So the two sons set out on their journey. They traveled for many days without finding water. Finally, they spotted a dead animal and ate some of the meat. The older brother stuffed himself, but the younger one ate only enough to fill himself. The older brother also decided to take some of the meat with him to eat along the way, but the younger son once again remembered his father's warning.

The younger son was surprised and disappointed that his brother was so blatantly disobeying their father, but he stayed with his older brother to try to find food and water for the family.

Eventually, the brothers found nomadic pastures, with water and food. The younger brother duly threw up the unclean meat in his stomach, and he remembered to wash himself before eating the food set out before them by a nomad family. But he refused to eat from the same plate as his brother, whom he regarded as unclean.

A little boy scoops up water, a precious commodity in Somalia and one often featured in poetry and stories.

The father was told this whole story when the two sons returned home. Gurgati was furious with his older son for disobeying and disgracing him, and cast him out from his house.

The older son became poorer and poorer, traveling from town to town in search of food and work. Eventually he got married and had children, and his children had children of their own, and so on, through the generations.

Today, the Somalis believe that the poor and laboring people of their country are descendants of this older son of Gurgati. The story ends on the note that although the two classes are separated by the acts of this son, all Somalis are one family united by religion and language.

TRADITION OF POETRY

Somalis have the gift of poetry, and the country's poetry is one of its greatest artistic achievements. For centuries, it has been not just an art form but also a political and cultural tool.

If a community was confronted with a problem, tribal leaders met to decide on what action to take. After a decision had been reached, the wise men passed it on to the local poet.

The poet, who commanded great respect in the community, would then compose a poem. Such a poem, bringing the decision of the leaders to the people, was called a *gabaye* ("gah-bah-YAH").

The town or village community would gather to hear the poem being delivered. The poet recited the *gabaye* only once to the community. Subsequent recitations were left to the poetry reciters.

Poems recited to those in villages and small towns often had the power to bring about important political changes and even to start a war or to end it.

RECITING IT PERFECTLY, WORD FOR WORD

A group known as the poetry reciters had the honored job of repeating the message given out by the village or town poet. These poetry reciters had to repeat the poem perfectly, word for word. They needed to have excellent memories, because the *gabaye* could be more than a hundred words long.

The *gabaye* was often able to influence people in a powerful way. Perhaps for this reason, poetry reciters were not allowed to make any facial expressions during their recitations, or act out the story in any way, or emphasize any words or phrases.

The poetry reciters' role was to repeat the poem not only to the poet's community, but to other communities as well, and always with perfect accuracy. Such poems would often include details of local history, current affairs, and the community's customs.

POEMS AND DANCES

Somalis also compose poems to commemorate various occasions in their private lives—to explain their feelings to someone they love, to propose a marriage or to end it, to celebrate the birth of a child, or to mourn the death of a loved one.

More public events that require the composing and recital of poetry may be conducted in the form of political debates in verse. Some of these public occasions may also call for dancers to perform. Somalis are not only fond of dancing, but they are good at improvising and at performing traditional dances.

But the art of verbal poetry may be in danger of fading away. The nomadic Somalis are beginning to learn to read and write, which means they no longer need to rely so exclusively on getting their information via the local poet and the poetry reciters. Radio broadcasting has also led to wider dissemination of information. Messages from one community to another can now be freely transmitted over the air waves.

Some Somali poets and authors are presently trying to collect all of the poems and stories in the oral tradition and write them down, to preserve this heritage for future generations. This written form of poems and tales may someday become the classical Somali literature.

JEWELRY AND ARTIFACTS

Somali men and women are fond of wearing ornamental jewelry on festive occasions. Silver is the preferred metal, as many Somalis believe that silver is the "pure" metal blessed by the Prophet Mohammed, and that gold belongs to the devil and brings bad luck.

Since few Somalis can afford even silver, most jewelry is made of colored beads of wood, stone, or glass.

The three different necklaces worn by this woman are typical of the work of Somali craftsworkers.

Traditionally Somali women make pottery without a potter's wheel. They take a ball of clay, hollow it out, and mold it into shape. Once the piece of pottery is baked, the women add dye from plants to create color and design.

Somalis, particularly the women, also make decorative cups of wood. Some of these wooden cups are used for drinking, but others are fashioned to hold powder and other cosmetic items. They tend to be well designed, featuring motifs of animals, boats, or huts.

Both men and women are adept at carving wood to make objects such as spoons or boxes for holding medicine, jewelry, and other accessories.

Although most rural Somalis eat their food with their right hand, they do have finely carved serving spoons, traditionally seen as a symbol of wealth. If a family possesses such spoons, they place them on the table to show that they are successful.

The spoon is also a symbol of domesticity. When a young woman gives birth to her first child, she is likely to receive a spoon to symbolize the

ROCK PAINTINGS AND OTHER FINDS

There are numerous archeological sites in Somalia, but few have been explored. In the north, burial sites containing bones, Stone-Age weapons, and domestic items have been discovered. Rock paintings and Stone-Age remains have also been uncovered along the northern coast.

Many of the rock paintings depict animals that are mythical or now extinct. Beneath each rock painting is an inscription, but scientists have not yet deciphered the meanings of this form of ancient writing. Many scientists believe that the rock paintings are over 2,500 years old.

In the Wadi Valley at Mudan, archeologists have found the ruins of a large town. In these ruins are the remains of three big mosques and about 2,000 tombs. In Las Anod, archeologists have located the remains of another city. More than 200 buildings, recognized as being built in the same style as the older part of Mogadishu, were found within this city. This indicates that the same types of people lived in Mogadishu and in Las Anod. Mogadishu has an old town called Hammawein, a central market, and a mosque dating from the 13th century.

new phase of her life. Most of these spoons are made of wood and have decorative handles. Some are made of silver or ivory, and rich urban Somalis use such spoons functionally rather than for display.

VARIED ARCHITECTURE

Traditional dwellings in the rural areas are small modest homes, the domed hut or *akal* being the most common. Architecture in the cities is more varied and may be ancient or modern, lavish or modest. Some are quaint structures from the past, many are bland stone buildings suitable for the hot climate, and yet others are modern buildings in the Western style.

It is unfortunate that within the last 10 years bombs and gunfire have destroyed much of the most historic and beautiful architecture of the cities of Somalia, especially those along the coast.

Modest stone facade of a building in Hammawein, an old quarter of Mogadishu.

93

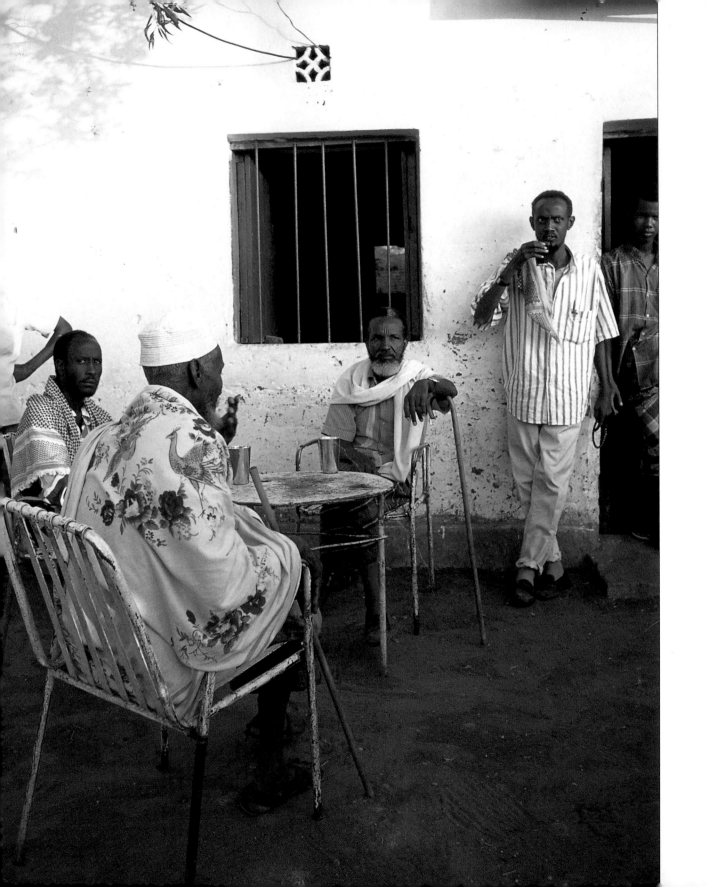

LEISURE

FAMINES AND CIVIL WARS have curtailed Somalis' enjoyment of leisure pastimes over the past decade, but they still take part in various activities whenever they can. In the north, the mountains provide opportunities for good hiking, rock climbing, and animal watching.

In the fertile region between the two main rivers, Somalis often go for a swim—although they have to watch out for predatory creatures such as crocodiles and alligators. Swimming is a bit safer on the coast, but even here, there is a danger of sharks if swimmers venture out too far.

In rural areas people tend to be sociable. Visiting neighbors in the clan community or gathering together for a session of making handicrafts are favorite pastimes for the women. The children enjoy playing games and listening to stories told by their elders. All across the country, Somalis engage in sports such as running, soccer, and boxing. Popular pastimes in the cities include going to theaters and cinemas.

Left: **The woman in the foreground has just been calling on her neighbors, a typical leisure activity for Somali women.**

Opposite: **Some men relaxing outside a coffee house.**

95

COFFEE BREAKS

Somali women meet each other as often as they can, usually in each others' homes or in stores. Until a few years ago, a Somali female seldom entered a restaurant. If she did, she was assumed to be a woman of ill repute. To avoid misunderstanding, Somali women still tend to avoid going into restaurants.

Whenever a Somali housewife finds herself with some time in the morning, she visits her friends and relatives. She stays to chat and to drink coffee or fruit juice. Half an hour for such a visit is considered long enough to be enjoyable but not intrusive.

Men in the towns and cities socialize mainly in restaurants and coffee houses. These places are full at all times of the day, with different groups of men eating, drinking coffee, or simply talking.

The amenities may be a bit lacking, but these Somalis make the most of their leisure time, drinking coffee at a friend's house.

GOING TO MARKET

All Somalis, especially the women, enjoy going to the market. It's where they do the family shopping, bump into friends, and get the chance to pick up some bargains. For rural women living far from a town, the trip to the market is a day-long event.

All Somali women do their marketing early in the morning. The outdoor markets are the best places to find fresh fruit and vegetables, as well as meat and milk. The vendors sit in the sun all day long to sell their goods.

When a Somali woman wants to buy milk, she brings along tin containers with handles. She goes tasting from vendor to vendor, and once she finds the milk she likes, she fills up all of her tins with the milk.

The marketplace is usually a square in the middle of town. In the larger towns and cities, little shops are located all round it. Somalis love to spend time examining the wares in these shops, selling mainly handicrafts.

In Mogadishu, the main market is on Soqaamadin Street, a coastal road by the Indian Ocean. The shops surrounding it display handicrafts made of camel bone, wood, or fabric.

LEATHERWORK AND WEAVING

Somalis have for centuries made beautiful handcrafted items. Traditional leather objects such as sandals, charms, cowhide beds, and pitchers for water and milk are crafted by those living in the rural communities. Hours are spent making intricate designs in leather. In the cities, leather goods are produced mainly in tanneries and leather factories.

During the colonial period, the Italians taught the Somalis modern leatherworking techniques and helped them build factories. Such factories now turn out decorative leather items such as purses, sandals, and jackets with fringes. They also produce coats and footwear from animal pelts, which are popular with the wealthier urban Somalis.

Somalis also enjoy weaving rugs from homemade cotton. To make the cotton, they remove the soft fluff from around the cotton seeds, spin the fluff into thread, and then weave lengths of cloth. They then dye the cloth and hang it up to dry, after which the weavers place the dry cloth onto a loom. To make mats involves a different process. First the women pull bark from the trees, pound it, and then chew it. Once the bark is soft, the women weave it into mats.

Other local products include pipes, candlesticks, beadwork, shell necklaces, small carvings, and products made from ivory and tortoiseshell.

Wealthy urban Somalis are fond of wearing coats made of leopard skin, but such items are no longer easy to obtain as leopard hunting has been prohibited.

GETTING INTO A SOMALI CINEMA WITH NO TICKET

Cinemas in Somalia tend to be of two kinds—an open-air theater consisting of long benches and a screen, or an enclosed hall typical of those in the West. At the cinema, women and children traditionally sit on the lower level, while the men occupy the upper level.

Purchasing a ticket at a Somali cinema used to be an interesting experience. First the person who wants to see a movie approaches the ticket-seller and hands over some money. The ticket-seller, clutching the money, then decides whether to give the person a ticket. Usually the customer is not given a ticket but is allowed into the cinema anyway. This was because the former Socialist government controlled the cinemas and required them to turn over all their profits. Cinema owners naturally were not pleased with this and used to tell their staff not to issue too many tickets, so that they did not have a record of having sold these tickets to customers. In this way, they kept most of their proceeds..

Somali children enjoy trips to the cinema and watching Western action movies, even if they do not understand the language. The children always cheer out loud for the Indians in cowboy-and-Indian movies—because they think that the Indians look a bit like them. Most Somali parents do not like their children to go to the cinema, as they do not approve of Western movies with too much sex and violence.

FUN ON THE BEACHES

Friday is the day off work for Somalis. On this day and on holidays, people take their families to the beaches, especially to those in Mogadishu. They play football, stroll by the ocean, run in the surf, or brave the shark-infested waters to swim. The children enjoy building sandcastles or playing games along the beach.

The most popular beach in Mogadishu is Gezira beach. The main hotel on Gezira beach protects its cove from sharks, so swimming is safe in this area. A number of exclusive coves along this beach ensure complete privacy, though these coves are not protected from sharks and swimming can be quite risky.

The waters of Somalia are also home to many other living creatures that make swimming less attractive than it would otherwise be. The scorpion fish is a beautiful, colorful fish with zebra-like stripes—and poisonous dorsal spines. This fish, unlike sharks, will not attack unless provoked. Another dangerous fish found in Somali waters is the stonefish, which looks like a piece of coral but has a poisonous venom.

GOING FOR GOLD

Over the past few decades, the country has become very involved in sports. Somalia has been a member of the International Athletics Federation since 1959, and many Somalis have competed in the Olympics since then.

A Somali athlete named Abdi Bileh won the first gold medal for his country in the 1987 World Athletic Championships in Rome. Many of the good athletes later leave Somalia to train abroad, since facilities in other countries are better.

Mogadishu has a large stadium for soccer games and other sports. Soccer, the world's most popular sport, is also highly popular in Somalia, both as a participatory and as a spectator sport, though Somalis call the game football.

Other favorite games that Somalis play include volleyball and water sports. American football and boxing attract good crowds of spectators.

Somali sportsmen and women are not as well recognized as those in neighboring Kenya, but they are doing their best to win more international medals.

A group of Somali boys playing soccer, or football as they prefer to call it.

CITY PLEASURES

The cities come alive at night when both men and women dress up for an evening on the town. A wide array of entertainment is on offer. Mogadishu has a popular disco in the basement of one of the larger hotels. Both locals and foreigners patronize the disco. Another popular night spot in Mogadishu is called Azan's.

Apart from going to bars and restaurants, Mogadishu residents enjoy watching a play or going to a poetry reading at the Mogadishu National Theater. At the weekend, going to the movies to see an American or European film is common.

Clubs where local Somali bands play African and European music are popular in the cities.

THE STARRY AFRICAN NIGHT

For centuries Somalis have been intrigued by the stars in the sky and have spent hours gazing at them. In most of Somalia, there is an absence of tall buildings and air pollution to cloud the sky. The nomads in the vast open countryside especially have an incredible view of a dark sky pitted with millions of bright stars. Many Somalis have gone into careers in astronomy and astrology, and a Somali named Musa Galal wrote a book called *The Terminology and Practice of Weather Lore, Astronomy and Astrology*, which brought him international fame.

Somalis not only enjoy gazing at the stars during their leisure time, but also plan important events in their life by the position of the stars and the moon. For instance, some Somalis will consult an astrologer before planning a wedding or an important vacation. If the astrologer predicts that the day is an unlucky one, then the Somali will postpone the event. If a boy is born during the new moon, which lasts for one to two nights each month, Somalis believe that the child is blessed. Society does not allow such a boy to shave his head at all, as his hair is believed to be holy.

RURAL ENTERTAINMENT

The nomads and other inhabitants of rural Somalia have their own traditional entertainment. The men have activities that tend to be different from the women's. They enjoy working in groups—caring for their flocks, raising crops, or hunting for food. The women enjoy visiting each other and cooking a meal together or making handicrafts. A daily trip to the market is a favorite activity.

An afternoon nap, or a siesta, is almost compulsory for both men and women, in both rural or urban areas. Somalis close their shops, leave their fields, or stop cooking when the siesta hour comes round. A siesta may last from 2 to 4.30 p.m. In the cities, people often leave their offices and go home to rest, then return for a few more hours of work.

Somalis believe that leisure activity is meant to be shared.

FESTIVALS

FESTIVALS ARE JOYOUS OCCASIONS in Somalia in which family, friends, and clan members gather together for feasts and merrymaking. Nearly all festivities have a religious significance, whether it is to celebrate a birth or marriage or to observe a public event.

The Muslim lunar calendar dictates the dates of the religious festivals in Somalia, as is the case in all other Islamic nations. Somalis celebrate the new year of the Muslim calendar with a festival called Muharram. During the first 10 days of the first month, three things are done: all Muslim Somalis tell the tale of the "Tree at the Boundary," while Shiite Muslims honor Prophet Mohammed's grandson Hussein and celebrate Ashura.

Other important celebrations are *Maulid an-Nabi* ("MAU-lid ahn-NAH-bee") and Ramadan. *Maulid an-Nabi* occurs on the 12th day of the third month, and Ramadan is observed throughout the ninth month.

Left: **These men, who belong to the same community, turned out in force for holiday celebrations.**

Opposite: **Somalis in festive mood as they parade en masse through the city streets.**

THE TREE AT THE BOUNDARY

All Muslims believe that on the first day of Muharram an angel shakes a tree at the boundary of earth and paradise. The tree represents the Muslim people, and each leaf represents an individual. The Somalis believe that if the leaf bearing an individual's name falls off, that person will die during the coming year.

Because the angel is the only being to see each falling leaf, no one knows whose time has come until the person actually dies. Therefore, when anyone dies, Somalis believe that the angel shook that person's leaf off the tree on the first day of Muharram.

OH HUSSEIN! OH HUSSEIN! The Prophet Mohammed had a grandson named Hussein who was killed in battle. The Muslims recount the story of his life and death every night during the first 10 days of Muharram. Often Somalis will shout, "Oh Hussein! Oh Hussein!" as they listen to their religious leaders telling the highly emotional story. For this reason, this honoring of the Prophet's grandson has come to be known as "Oh Hussein! Oh Hussein!"

It is during the daylight hours of Muharram that the Somalis honor Hussein. They reenact important events in his life by assuming various roles and acting the parts exactly as has been told in history.

CALENDAR OF SOMALI HOLIDAYS

National Holidays

January 1	New Year's Day
May 1	Labor Day
June 26	Independence of Somaliland
July 1	Independence of the Somali Republic
October 21-22	Anniversary of the 1969 Revolution

Religious Holidays

Month 1, days 1-10	Muharram
Month 1, day 1	The Tree at the Boundary
Month 1, days 1-9	Oh Hussein! Oh Hussein!
Month 1, day 10	Ashura
Month 3, day 12	Mohammed's Birthday (Maulid an-Nabi)
Month 9	Ramadan
Month 10, first day	Id al-Fitr
Month 12, day 10	Id al-Adha

Christian Holidays

April (specific Sunday)	Easter
December 25	Christmas

Somalis believe that a person who dies while fasting during Ramadan does so with Allah's blessing.

DAY OF ASHURA The 10th day of Muharram is called Ashura. It represents the end of the mourning period for Hussein and the beginning of celebrations for the perpetuation of humankind, as represented by the saving of Noah and his family during the 40 days of the deluge. Somali children in particular are fond of listening to this account of Noah and the great flood.

Muslims, like Christians and Jews, believe that God directed Noah to build an ark, and that Noah was then told to bring two specimens of every bird and beast, male and female, into his ark. In this way, Noah's family and the birds and beasts of the earth were kept alive during the deluge that destroyed the rest of humankind.

On the day of Ashura, Somali men reenact the death of Hussein. At nightfall everyone in the neighborhood gathers to attend a feast.

BIRTHDAY OF THE PROPHET

On the 12th day of the third month of the Muslim lunar calendar, the day of *Maulid an-Nabi,* Somalis celebrate the birth of the Prophet Mohammed. The village or the family gather together to listen to stories and legends about this very special event.

According to legend, 7,000 angels brought heavenly mist to earth inside a golden urn. This urn was presented to Mohammed's mother when she was giving birth to her son. As the baby appeared, every living creature proclaimed, "There is no God but Allah, and Mohammed is His Prophet." The angels then bathed the newborn Mohammed in the heavenly mist to perpetuate eternal cleanliness.

HOLY MONTH OF RAMADAN Muslims all over the world observe a month of fasting during Ramadan, the ninth month of the Islamic calendar. Somali Muslims fast from dawn to dusk throughout the month.

They believe firmly in fasting. It is a means by which they can truly show devotion to Allah and to Mohammed. They also believe it builds self-discipline and enables them to show compassion to the less fortunate. Since Ramadan is determined by the Muslim lunar calendar, it takes place at a somewhat different time each year. If Somalis have to fast during a cool rainy period, they find it fairly tolerable. But during a hot dry period, they have a tough time spending an entire day without water.

It is common for the sick and elderly to fall sick and die if Ramadan occurs during the hot months, but Somalis and Muslims all over the world consider it an honor to die during Ramadan.

BREAKING THE FAST

On the last day of Ramadan, the Somalis break their fast. This festival is called *Id al-Fitr* ("EED ahl-Fee-TEHR"), and lasts for three days. The Somalis celebrate by feasting and spending the money that they have saved during the year. Wealthy urban Somalis invite their friends and families to their homes for feasts. The rural Somalis feast with the other village members.

Women carrying firewood back to the village in preparation for the cooking and feasting that will take place on the last day of Ramadan.

The last Muslim holiday during the lunar year is called *Id al-Adha* ("EED ahl-ah-DAH"). On this day, Somali Muslims remember how Abraham nearly sacrificed his son Ishmael, celebrating the event as signifying Abraham's love for Allah.

They tell of how Allah told Abraham that he could prove his devotion by sacrificing his son. It was heartbreaking for Abraham, but he prepared to do God's bidding. At the moment that he was raising the knife to kill Ishmael, Allah ordered him to stop. This was because Abraham had already shown his devotion to Allah. On *Id al-Adha*, Somali Muslims visit the graves of their relatives and bring food to the less fortunate.

THREE-DAY WEDDINGS

Wedding festivities may last for three days, especially if the family of the bride is able to afford such a party. For three days and three nights before the wedding ceremony, friends and family members go to the bride's home for dancing, drinking, and eating.

The first two days and nights of the wedding festivities are attended mostly by the younger generation, but on the last night, everyone concerned will be there, and the dancing goes on until midnight.

When it is time for the newlyweds to depart for their new life together, the bride leaves the party with an older woman who helps her shower and put on new clothes. If the couple is well-off, they then drive off to another city for their honeymoon. All the guests follow them in cars to a halfway point in their journey. At this midpoint, everyone gets out of their cars, and dancing and singing go on until the early hours of the morning.

In accordance with the Muslim faith, Somalis do not touch alcohol even on highly festive occasions.

At weddings, merry-making and dancing often go on until late at night.

CIRCUMCISION CEREMONIES

Both male and female Somali children are circumcised, and festivities surround these events. The parents invite all their friends, relatives, and neighbors for a feast after the child's circumcision ceremony. To prepare for this feast, the women of the household will cook all night, killing as many animals as necessary.

A young girl who has to undergo the ordeal of circumcision has to first take a shower. The women in her family prepare for the ceremony by wrapping old scarves around their shoulders and shaving their heads. A religious leader then reads out parts of the Koran, and the circumcision takes place.

After that people come into the house in small groups to partake of the food and to fumigate their hair with incense smoke. Others wait outside, singing and dancing until it is their turn to enter the house.

Everyone in this group is likely to have been circumcised. Feasts and celebrations are held to commemorate the event, but circumcision is a painful ordeal for the young girls of Somalia.

FOOD

THE STAPLES OF THE SOMALI DIET are rice, bananas, and the meat of sheep or goat. Corn and beans are also grown and eaten.

Because parts of the country came under Italian rule for so long, many Somalis eat pasta, such as spaghetti and macaroni, as a staple food. The local bread of Somalia is called *muufo* ("moo-OO-foh"), which is a flat bread somewhat like pita bread.

The nomadic groups raise livestock of sheep, goats, and cattle to sell to the rest of the population, but they also depend on these animals as a source of food. That was why during the years of famine in Somalia between the late 1970s and early 1990s, these nomads suffered so greatly. Not only was their means of livelihood lost when their animals died during droughts and floods, but meat and milk from their cattle were no longer available to them.

Somalis also eat the meat of camels, which they consider to be a delicacy. A Somali family only serves camel meat at a meal if they are expecting important guests.

The one meat that Somalis will not eat or touch is pork. The Muslim faith forbids its followers from eating pork because the eating habits of pigs are regarded as unclean.

Below: **A Somali butcher at work.**

Opposite: **A woman sieving a tray of corn.**

SOMALI KITCHENS

In many areas of Somalia, kitchens often have no running water or electricity. In the cities there are modern kitchens with the latest fittings and electronic appliances. As a result of the civil wars of the 1990s, even homes in the cities lost their electricity and running water. People were forced to prepare food with impure water, which resulted in serious illnesses and deaths.

In the countryside many homes do not have a kitchen. Rural living quarters are usually big enough only for a few beds. This is especially true of the nomads, whose mobile homes serve only as sleeping quarters.

Rural Somalis prepare their food outdoors, or inside a central village hut. The village women often gather together to prepare corn porridge in the mornings. They set up a tin bucket, add the corn and water, and pound the mixture with a stick.

In contrast, there are well-off urban Somalis who have been unaffected by the civil wars. This small privileged group have modern kitchens and often even a chef to prepare the family meals. Apart from the cooking, these chefs are usually required to do the marketing and serve the food.

STARVATION IN SOMALIA

The famine of the 1990s hit the rural Somalis particularly hard; many of them were forced to leave their homes to obtain food and shelter in the refugee camps. It is therefore sad but unavoidable that a chapter on the food of Somalia has to include a reminder of how thousands of Somalis died of starvation and malnutrition only recently.

These women and the little girl had no choice but to live on food handouts from relief organizations during the famine of the early 1990s.

At the refugee camps, starving Somalis received food rations that had been donated by various countries. When international volunteers at the overcrowded camps were giving out food, the Somalis had no choice but to jostle and even struggle with each other for handouts of a bowl of rice or a piece of meat.

Those Somalis who stayed put in their homes went through the painful process of watching their livestock die from malnutrition. Because Somalis have a respect for their camels, watching these animals die was agonizing for them.

Rather than depend on the refugee camps, many decided to travel around the countryside in search of food and water for their families and livestock. Most of these nomads ended up dying from lack of food.

Due to the worldwide publicity given to the various famines, many still think of Somalia as a land without food.

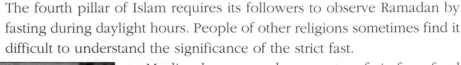

WHY SOMALIS FAST

The fourth pillar of Islam requires its followers to observe Ramadan by fasting during daylight hours. People of other religions sometimes find it difficult to understand the significance of the strict fast.

This array of grains and spices is what a local market stall has to offer.

Muslims have several reasons to refrain from food and water during Ramadan. In addition to enabling them to demonstrate their love and devotion to Allah, Somali Muslims believe that fasting enables them to clear their minds and focus on religion, family, and personal goals. They also believe that fasting allows them to develop an understanding for those who do not have enough food to eat.

Unfortunately, in recent years many Somali Muslims did not have to fast to know exactly how it felt to go without food for days and even weeks.

TIME FOR FEASTS

At the end of Ramadan, Somalis express their joy by feasting. Food is usually plentiful at such times, with generous servings of meat, vegetables, homemade bread, and rice. Friends, families, neighbors, and the poor are invited to the feast.

Somalis also eat well on other occasions such as festivals, birthdays, weddings, and circumcisions. Amid the general feasting, there will be dancing, storytelling, and singing.

Preparing for these feasts is also an enjoyable experience for Somali women. They make the trip to the local market and buy what food they need, perhaps even one or two handcrafted items. A market may have hundreds of stalls selling fruit, vegetables, meat, rice, bread, coffee, tea, and milk.

The vendors who sell charcoal at these colorful markets are well patronized, as most rural Somali women cook using charcoal for fuel.

SITTING DOWN TO EAT

It is customary for Somali men and women to eat separately. The women prepare the food and serve the men, and only after the menfolk had finished eating would the women sit down to eat with the children. Even in the cities it was not the accepted practice for women to eat together with men in restaurants until recently.

Women and girls prepare the meals together in the rural areas. If meat is going to be on the table, then the young boys of the family are often sent out to pick out the sheep or goat to be slaughtered.

Everyone gathers together once the meal is ready, sitting at a big table to eat.

After the meal, the older boys and girls of the village often collect wood to build a big fire. Then they will dance together around the fire. The fire not only provides light but also keeps away the flies and mosquitoes.

For the youngsters, such "campfire" activities are as much a part of the meal as the eating itself.

Two women cooking in an indoor kitchen. Preparing a meal often brings the women together.

117

A salad on the menu of a Mogadishu restaurant.

EATING OUT

The cities of Somalia offer a wide variety of food in their restaurants. Fancy restaurants are inexpensive by Western standards. A good three-course meal costs about $10 per person.

A meal at the cheapest restaurants costs between $2 and $5. And even better value is the food from street vendors, which can be bought hot for immediate consumption for less than $2.

Although such prices seem cheap to the people of other nations, the value of the Somali shilling is rather low, so that a few U.S. dollars can represent a lot of money to a Somali.

During the month of Ramadan, almost all restaurants in Somalia remain closed until sundown. The few restaurants that remain open during the day are usually owned by non-Muslim Somalis.

Some of the restaurants in the big cities, especially in Mogadishu, offer cuisines from other countries, such as Chinese, Italian, Middle Eastern, and even American-style foods.

Some Mogadishu restaurants and those in other coastal cities offer fresh fish and lobster caught by Somali fishermen that very day.

Because of the strong Arabic influence after the seventh century, many of the city restaurants sell traditional Arabic food such as kebabs (skewers of grilled lamb and vegetables).

THE CUP THAT REFRESHES

Favorite Somali drinks are coffee and tea, which are often served before or after a meal. This is because some Muslims do not like to mix their food and drink. Somalis prefer to grind their own freshly roasted coffee beans rather than buy ready-ground coffee. They may drink their coffee black, or add milk and sugar.

The Somalis serve tea in several different ways, one of which is to add lots of milk and sugar to produce a milky tea. They also drink their tea plain or add fresh fruit for extra flavor.

Islam forbids its followers to drink alcoholic beverages, so devout Somali Muslims do not drink alcohol, although there are some who enjoy an occasional glass of beer or wine.

Somalia produces its own rum, which is enjoyed by Somalis and visitors to the country. Somalis also consume a lot of water, especially during the hot months, as well as canned or bottled carbonated drinks.

FRESH LOCAL FARE

People in each of the four regions of Somalia tend to favor their own local produce, which is fresher and more readily available to them. Those along the coast, for instance, eat a lot of fresh fish, while the nomads eat the meat of sheep, goats, and cattle, and rarely have fish.

The people along the rivers often eat crocodile and alligator meat, along with fresh vegetables.

This man is taking time off to enjoy his glass of coffee.

119

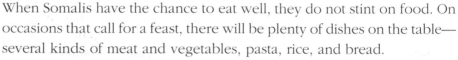

UNUSUAL FAVORITES

When Somalis have the chance to eat well, they do not stint on food. On occasions that call for a feast, there will be plenty of dishes on the table—several kinds of meat and vegetables, pasta, rice, and bread.

One favorite dish, especially at breakfast, is fried liver with onions and

Bread sellers on a side street. The favorite Somali bread is called *muufo,* **which resembles pita bread.**

bread. This may not seem so unusual, except that it may be camel's liver that appears on the table. More commonly, it is fried liver of sheep or goat that is served.

Somalis are very fond of marinara sauce, which is of Italian origin and made of tomatoes, onions, garlic, and spices. The sauce was a coveted food item during the famine years, and families considered themselves well-fed if they could afford a can of marinara sauce to eat with pasta once a week.

Muufo is the most popular bread among Somalis. Many make a living baking it and selling it to market stallholders and others. The corn for *muufo* is first ground into flour. Yeast, salt, oils, and water are added. The dough is slapped repeatedly until it is fairly flat, then placed in a clay oven over hot coals. Once the bread is done, the baker reaches a hand into an aperture in the oven to pull out the loaf. For this reason, Somalis who make *muufo* often have burns and scars on their arms and hands.

LIVER AND ONIONS

1 cup milk
$^1/_2$ cup flour
1–2 pounds ($^1/_2$–1 kg) sliced liver of beef, goat, or camel
4 tablespoons butter or shortening
2 medium onions, sliced into rings

Combine the milk and flour. Dip the strips of liver in the mixture and place in a frying pan containing 3 of the 4 tablespoons of butter or shortening. Fry liver strips for 2 to 3 minutes until slightly pink in the center.
Move liver to the side of the pan. Add remaining butter or shortening, then onion rings, frying them until brown. For extra flavor, add a small amount of lemon juice with water. Serve with warm bread.

TABLE MANNERS

When Somalis are about to eat a meal, they first wash their hands in a large bowl of soapy water. For a family meal in the rural areas, the father sits down and serves himself by reaching into the serving bowl with a spoon or with his right hand.

Next, the children help themselves. If their mother is sitting down to eat with them, she serves herself first and then her sons. She uses her right hand or a serving spoon to dole out the food.

Rural Somalis often eat with their fingers. When picking up food with their right hand, Somalis use only the first three fingers.

When rural Somalis venture into the cities, they have a difficult time trying to eat with a knife and fork. The Western style of eating is something the urbanized Somalis are more used to doing.

But eating with one's hand is not considered ill-mannered. Even in the cities, people commonly eat with their hands. Many African Muslims, including the Somalis, believe that for a meal to be truly enjoyed, it has to be eaten with one's hand.

The left hand is never used for eating, as this is the "unclean" hand in the Muslim tradition. It is the hand that Muslims use for ablutions and is never used to bring food to the mouth.

A banana leaf rolled up into a cone serves Somalis as a scoop for taking up food with a sauce.

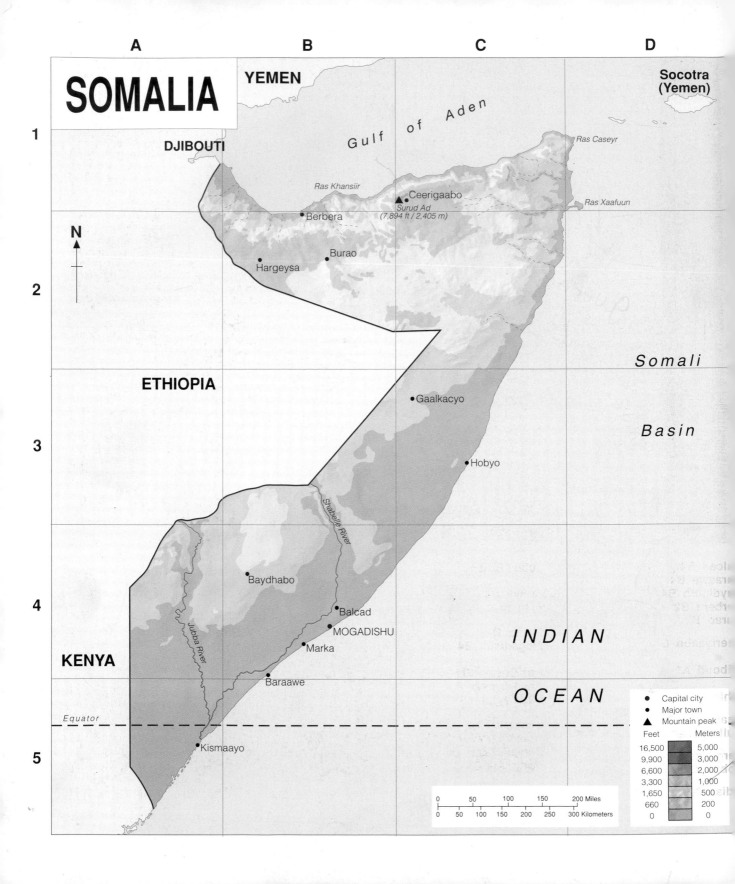

SOMALIA

YEMEN

Socotra
(Yemen)

DJIBOUTI

Gulf of Aden

Ras Caseyr

N

Ras Khansiir

Ceerigaabo

Ras Xaafuun

▲ Surud Ad
(7,894 ft / 2,405 m)

Berbera

Burao

Hargeysa

ETHIOPIA

Somali

• Gaalkacyo

Basin

• Hobyo

Shabelle River

Baydhabo

Balcad

MOGADISHU

INDIAN

Jubba River

Marka

KENYA

Baraawe

OCEAN

Equator

Kismaayo

• Capital city
• Major town
▲ Mountain peak

Feet		Meters
16,500		5,000
9,900		3,000
6,600		2,000
3,300		1,000
1,650		500
660		200
0		0

0	50	100	150	200 Miles
0	50	100	150	200	250	300 Kilometers

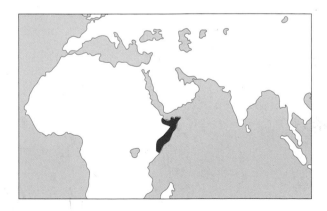

QUICK NOTES

OFFICIAL NAME
Somali Democratic Republic

TERM FOR CITIZENS
Somalis

AREA
246,090 square miles (637,370 square km)

POPULATION
8,050,000

CAPITAL
Mogadishu

MAIN CITIES
Marka, Kismaayo, Hargeysa, Berbera

MOUNTAIN RANGES
Oogo and Golis

HIGHEST POINT
Surud Ad (7,894 feet / 2,405 meters)

MAJOR RIVERS
Shabelle and Jubba

CLIMATE
Hot and dry, with rainy seasons from April to June and October to November. Temperatures range from 86–104°F (30–40°C) to 32°F (0°C).

CURRENCY
Shilling
(US$ = 1 shilling)

MAIN EXPORTS
Livestock, bananas, corn, beans

FORM OF GOVERNMENT
Independent republic

OFFICIAL LANGUAGE
Somali

NATIONAL FLAG
Five-pointed star

NATIONAL SYMBOL
The leopard

MAJOR RELIGION
Islam

SECTS OF ISLAM
Most Somalis are Sunni Muslims
The sects within the Sunni branch: Qadiriya, Salihiya, Ahmediya

MUSLIM HOLIDAYS
Muharram
Ramadan
Maulid an-Nabi
Id al-Fitr
Id al-Adha

LEADERS IN GOVERNMENT
Aden Abdullah Osman: first president
Abdi Rashid Ali Shermarke: first prime minister and then president from 1967 to 1969
Mohammed Siad Barre: president from 1969 to 1991

GLOSSARY

akal ("ah-KAHL")
Nomadic homes made from hides and flexible sticks.

arish ("AH-reesh")
Rectangular home built of timber, mud, dung, and straw, with pitched tin or thatched roof.

baraca ("bah-RAH-kah")
Rectangular home with cement floors and timber walls.

baruka ("bah-ROO-kah")
Power believed to be God-given, enabling the possessor to bless or curse individuals.

Candho-qoy ("KAHN-doh-koy")
Literally, "the place of moist udders" of the camel.

casa matoni ("KAH-sa mah-TOH-nee")
A *baraca* with stone or cement walls.

casa moro ("KAH-sa MOH-roh")
A two-story stone home built in an Arab style.

dik-dik
Small antelope that lives in northern Somalia and along the major rivers.

gabaye ("gah-bah-YAH")
A poem composed to convey to the people of a community important decisions of tribal leaders.

geel-weyta ("GEEL-WEY-tah")
Literally "the place that weakens animals."

guntina ("goon-TEE-nah")
Long, colorful cloth that Somali women wrap around their bodies.

Haud
Geographic region extending across the width of Somalia from Hargeysa in the north to Gaalkacyo in the south, with lush vegetation during the rainy seasons.

hoopoe
Pinkish-brown bird with black and white stripes native to Somalia.

layis ("LAH-yis")
Exercises in a school textbook or the "breaking of a young camel."

muufo ("moo-OO-foh")
Somali bread, a flat bread resembling pita.

raadra ("RAAH-drah")
Conduct research; literally, "trace lost animals."

Somalfish
Government agency set up in the 1970s to promote the fishing industry.

zar ("Zahr")
Evil spirit supposedly invading the souls of women who harbor grievances against their husbands.

BIBLIOGRAPHY

Barnes, Virginia Lee. *Aman: The Story of a Somali Girl*, Pantheon Books, New York, 1994.

Godbeer, Deardre. *Somalia*, Chelsea House Publishers, New York, 1988.

Henze, Paul B. *The Horn of Africa*, MacMillan, London, 1991.

Hodd, Michael (editor). *East African Handbook*, Passport Books, Illinois, 1995.

Hudson, Peter. *A Leaf in the Wind: Travels in Africa*, Walker and Company, New York, 1988.

Laitan, David D. and Said S. Samatar. *Somalia: Nation in Search of a State*, Westview Press, Boulder, Colorado, 1987.

Lewis, I.M. *The Modern History of Somaliland*, Frederick A. Praeger, Publishers, New York, 1965.

Nelson, Harold D. (editor). *Somalia: A Country Study*, United States Government, 1982.

Sahnoun, Mohamed. *Somalia: The Missed Opportunities*, United States Institute of Peace Press, Washington, D.C., 1994.

INDEX

INDEX

INDEX

political groups, 25, 26–27, 32, 33, 35, 82
population, 11, 16–17, 42, 47, 51

radio, 45, 91
rainfall, 7, 9, 10, 11, 12, 16, 28, 36
Ramadan, 70, 105, 107, 108–109, 116, 118
refugee camps, 28, 55, 64, 115
relief organizations, 28, 64, 115
restaurants, 118
rivers
    Jubba, 7, 9, 12, 13, 15, 16, 25, 49, 50
    Shabelle, 7, 9, 12, 13, 16, 25, 49, 50, 75
rock paintings, 93

saints, 70, 74
Saudi Arabia, 33, 43, 70, 73, 80
Shermarke, Abdi Rashid Al, 31, 32
slaves, 19, 21
Socialism, 34, 39, 40, 50, 66, 76, 77, 99
Somalfish, 41
Somaliland, British, 9, 11, 17, 23, 24, 25, 27, 40, 87
Somaliland, Italian, 22, 26–27, 87
Soviet Union, 3, 32, 33, 41, 44, 58
sports, 95, 101
storytelling, 13, 15, 74, 88–89, 91

table manners, 121
television, 45
theater, 95
trading, 19, 21, 85
transportation, 14, 40, 44–45
"Tree at the Boundary," the 105, 106, 107

Ujuuraan, 21
United Nations, 25, 29, 35, 36, 37, 39, 61, 80
United States, 33, 34–35, 41, 58

wars
    civil war, 3, 29, 31, 34, 35, 36, 37, 47, 48, 58, 63, 64, 65, 95
    Ogaden War, 33
    World War I, 23
    World War II, 11, 24, 25, 26, 44
weaving, 85, 98–99
women, 28, 39, 43, 47, 53, 56, 57, 59, 60–61, 64, 67, 77, 83, 85, 92, 93, 95, 96, 97, 99, 103, 109, 110, 111, 113, 114, 116–117

Yeshaq, 20

DATE DUE
